Report of the Steering Group on

Foreign Direct Investment

PLANNING COMMISSION, GOVERNMENT OF INDIA

Report of the Steering Group on

Foreign Direct Investment

FDI

सत्यमेव जयते

Planning Commission

GOVERNMENT OF INDIA

NEW DELHI

August 2002

Published by

ACADEMIC FOUNDATION

NEW DELHI

Published in 2003 by
ACADEMIC FOUNDATION
4772-73 / 23 Bharat Ram Road,
(23 Ansari Road), Darya Ganj,
New Delhi - 110 002. INDIA.

Phones : 23245001, 02, 03, 04.
Fax : 011-23245005
e-mail : academic@vsnl.com
www : academicfoundation.com

Report of the Steering Group on Foreign Direct Investment
(Planning Commission, Government of India)

ISBN 81-7188-312-5

Printed at Print Perfect, Mayapuri Industrial Area, New Delhi.

Contents

Acronyms

ADRs	American Depository Receipts
ATK	AT Kearney
BCG	Boston Consulting Group
BOP	Balance of Payments
CAD	Current Account Deficit
CCFI	Cabinet Committee on Foreign Investment
CENVAT	Central Value Added Tax
CII	Confederation of Indian Industries
CPM	Critical Path Method
Crore	10 million
CRR	Cash Reserve Ratio
CST	Central Sales Tax
CVD	Countervailing Duties
DC	Developing Countries
DGFT	Director General of Foreign Trade
DIPP	Department of Industrial Policy & Promotion
DTA	Domestic Tariff Area
EAU	Entrepreneurial Assistance Unit
EIU	Economic Intelligence Unit
EOU	Export Oriented Units
EPZs	Export Promotion Zones
FDI	Foreign Direct Investment
FEMA	Foreign Exchange Management Act
FIAS	Foreign Investment Advisory Services
FICCI	Federation of Indian Chambers of Commerce & Industry

FIIA	Foreign Investment Implementation Authority
FII	Foreign Institutional Investors
FIPB	Foreign Investment Promotion Board
FIPC	Foreign Investment Promotion Council
FPO	Food Price Order
FTZs	Foreign Trade Zones
GDP	Gross Domestic Product
GDRs	Global Depository Receipts
GOI	Government of India
GOM	Group of Ministers
IATA	International Air Traffic Association
ICAMT	International Centre for Advancement of Manufacturing Technology
ICOR	Incremental Capital-Output Ratio
IDRA	Industries Development & Regulation Act
IEM	Industrial Entrepreneurs Memorandum
IFC	International Financial Corporation
ILDP	Indian Leather Development Programme
IMF	International Monetary Fund
IPAs	(State) Investment Promotion Agencies
IPO	Initial Public Offering
IT	Information Technology
JBIC	Japan Exim Bank
LNG	Liquefied Natural Gas
M&A	Mergers & Acquisitions
MAT	Minimum Alternate Tax
MES	Minimum Efficient Scale
MIDA	Malaysian Industrial Development Authority
MNC	Multinational Corporations
MNEs	Multinational Enterprises
MRTP	Monopolies & Restrictive Trade Practices
NBFCs	Non-Banking Financial Corporations

NCAER	National Council of Applied Economic Research
NFEE	Net Foreign Exchange Earning
NLDP	National Leather Development Programme
NRI	Non-Resident Indian
OCBs	Overseas Corporate Bodies
OECD	Organization of Economic Cooperation & Development
PERT	Project Evaluation Research Technique
PM	Prime Minister
RBI	Reserve Bank of India
RCA	Rent Control Acts
RIS	Research and Information System for the Non-Aligned and Other Developing Countries
S.E. Asia	South-East Asia
SEBI	Securities & Exchange Board of India
SEZ	Special Economic Zone
SIA	Secretariat for Industrial Assistance
SLR	Statutory Liquidity Ratio
SMEs	Small & Medium Enterprises
SSI	Small Scale Industries
ST	Sales Tax
TNCs	Transnational Corporations
TRAI	Telecom Regulatory Authority of India
TRIMS	Trade Related Investment Measures
ULCA	Urban Land Ceiling Acts
UN	United Nations
UNCTAD	United Nations Council for Trade and Development
UNIDO	United Nations Industrial Development Organisation
USO	Universal Service Obligation
VCCs	Venture Capital Companies

1

Preface

1.1 Committee Members

Foreign Direct Investment is one of the key variables for achieving an eight per cent growth during the Tenth Plan (2002-07). As mentioned in the Approach Paper a sharp step up in FDI is necessary for achieving the growth targets of the Tenth Plan. The Planning Commission constituted a *Steering Committee on Foreign Direct Investment* in August 2001, to achieve these objectives. The Steering Committee comprises the following members:

Shri N.K. Singh, *Member, Planning Commission*	**Chairman**
Shri Ajit Kumar, *Finance Secretary, Ministry of Finance*	Member
Shri V. Govindarajan, *Secretary (DIPP), Ministry of Commerce & Industry*	Member
Shri Shashank, *Secretary (ER), Ministry of External Affairs*	Member
Dr. Y.V. Reddy, *Deputy Governor, Reserve Bank of India*	Member
Shri A.P. Verma, *Chief Secretary, Government of Uttar Pradesh*	Member
Shri P.V. Rao, *Chief Secretary, Government of Andhra Pradesh*	Member

Shri Manish Gupta, *Chief Secretary, Government of West Bengal*	Member
Shri Prodipto Ghosh, *Additional Secretary, Prime Minister's Office*	Member
Shri Tarun Das, *Director General, CII*	Member
Dr. Amit Mitra, *Secretary General, FICCI*	Member
Dr. Arvind Virmani *Adviser (DP), Planning Commission*	Member-Secretary

Mr. C.M. Vasudev, Secretary (DEA) replaced Mr. Ajit Kumar on relinquishing charge as finance secretary.

1.2 Terms of Reference

The terms of reference of the Committee were as follows:

a. To suggest policy and governance reforms necessary for attracting private investment, both domestic and foreign.

b. To identify factors which inhibit higher FDI flows and suggest remedial steps.

c. To examine policy reforms towards mergers and acquisition for attracting FDI.

d. To suggest changes in institutional apparatus and organizations, both in Centre and States, for attracting the FDI flows.

e. To suggest Policy reforms in Export Processing Zones for attracting higher FDI flows.

f. To suggest policy and governance reforms to attract NRIs for making higher FDI.

g. To examine the factors responsible for the success of other countries like China in attracting FDI and make suitable recommendations based on the experience of other successful countries.

1.3 Acknowledgements

Dr. Sharat Kumar, Director, Development Policy Division, Planning Commission assisted the Steering Group in its work. Mrs. A. Srija, Senior Research Officer, Planning Commission also provided assistance in preparing the report.

2

Introduction

2.1 Background

Foreign Direct Investment (FDI) flows are usually preferred over other forms of external finance because they are non-debt creating, non-volatile and their returns depend on the performance of the projects financed by the investors. FDI also facilitates international trade and transfer of knowledge, skills and technology. In a world of increased competition and rapid technological change, their complimentary and catalytic role can be very valuable (Appendix section 8.1).

Foreign Direct Investment in India has constituted 1 per cent of Gross fixed capital formation in 1993, which went up to 4 per cent in 1997. The Tenth Plan approach paper postulates a GDP growth rate of 8 per cent during 2002-07. Given the Incremental Capital-Output Ratio (ICOR) and the projected level of domestic savings it leaves a savings gap/ current account deficit of around 2.2 per cent. This implies an increase in FDI from the present levels of $ 3.9 billion in 2001-02 to at least around US$ 8 billion a year during 2002-07 (Appendix section 8.2).

2.2 Meetings

The Steering Committee on FDI had eight meetings. In the first meeting of the Committee held on 6th September 2001 it was decided that the Steering Committee should come up with practical suggestions, which will help in achieving a higher levels of FDI inflow into India during the Tenth Plan. In the second and third meetings, leading consultancy firms and representatives from Chambers of Commerce were invited to make presentations of their surveys/analysis on FDI inflows into India (Appendix section 8.6.1 to 8.6.5). The fourth meeting had presentations from the State Governments (Appendix section 8.6.6). This was followed by a presentation by Department of Industrial Policy and Promotion (DIPP) at the fifth meeting (Appendix section 8.6.7). The sixth and seventh meeting discussed the issues connected with sectoral caps, entry/exit barriers and other policy issues. The eighth meeting finalised the recommendations of the committee.

2.3 Presentations

Among the consultancy groups and leading Chambers of Commerce that made presentations were McKinsey & Co., AT Kearney, Boston Consulting Group (BCG), FICCI and CII. According to BCG most of the foreign investment proposals get cut off at the screening stage. They recommend *'a rifle shot approach'* wherein the potential investors are short-listed and their concerns addressed. The FICCI presentation emphasised upon the role of archaic legislations and labour laws, unhelpful bureaucracy etc. in causing time and cost overruns. They suggested urgent initiatives for fast track clearance of legal disputes and improvement in bureaucratic mind set. CII highlighted the low levels of realization of FDI inflows vis-à-vis the proposals cleared. CII also suggested single window clearance of FDI proposals based on the Malaysian Industrial Development Authority (MIDA) model, for overcoming post-approval procedural delay. McKinsey & Co. divided FDI into three categories: domestic oriented, privatisation or disinvestment related and export related. It recommended sector specific measures to improve FDI inflows. AT Kearney & Co. identified bureaucracy as the top most concern of foreign investors. It pointed to India's skilled labour force as the country's most alluring attraction for foreign direct investors.

The government of Andhra Pradesh made a presentation on its new Act relating to Infrastructure Investment which has an inbuilt fast track mechanism. The government of West Bengal also made a presentation on their approach to FDI. The Department of Industrial Policy and Promotion (DIPP) also made a presentation to the Committee (Summary at Appendix section 8.6.7).

2.4 Material Collected

The Steering Committee received material from the Department of Industrial Policy & Promotion, Department of Commerce, Ministry of External affairs, NCAER and Administrative Staff College of India. It also examined other available literature on FDI brought forth by UNCTAD, World Bank and RIS.

3

FDI Trends

3.1 Global Trends

Global foreign direct investment (FDI) almost quadrupled between 1995 and 2000. However, FDI flows to developing countries grew at a much slower rate over this period, doubling to $ 240.2 billion their share (Table 3.1). FDI inflows into developing countries virtually halted in 1998 as a result of the Asian crisis. The share of developing countries in global flows reached a peak of 39.6 per cent in 1996, declining rapidly thereafter to reach 18.9 per cent of total flows in 2000 (Figure 3.1). Though absolute FDI amounts have declined in 2001, the share of developing countries has increased dramatically to 30 per cent.

TABLE – 3.1

FDI Inflows by Host Regions

(US $ Billion)

	1989-94 (ann.avg)	1995	1996	1997	1998	1999	2000	2001
I. World	200.1	331.1	384.9	477.9	692.5	1075.0	1270.8	760
II. Developed Countries	137.1	203.5	219.7	271.4	483.2	829.8	1005.2	500
III. Developing Countries	59.6	113.3	152.5	187.4	188.4	222.0	240.2	225
Share (%)	29.8	34.2	39.6	39.2	27.2	20.7	18.9	29.6

Source : World Investment Report, 2001 & UNCTAD Press Release of 21st January 2002.

3.2 India's Share

India's share in FDI inflows among developing countries reached a peak of 1.9 per cent in 1997. It declined sharply to 1 per cent in 1999 and 2000 but has recovered sharply to 1.7 per cent in 2001(Table 3.2). India's performance on the FDI front has shown a significant improvement since last year. FDI inflows grew by 65 per cent to US$ 3.91 billion during 2001-02 thus exceeding the previous peak of US$ 3.56 billion in 1997-98 (as per BOP accounts of RBI). This growth of 65 per cent is particularly encouraging at a time when global FDI inflows have declined by over 40 per cent.[1] The upward trend in FDI inflows has been sustained during the current financial year with FDI inflows during April-June 2002 about double that during the corresponding period of 2001 (as per DIPP data).[2]

Figure 3.1 : FDI Inflows by Host Regions: Amount and Share

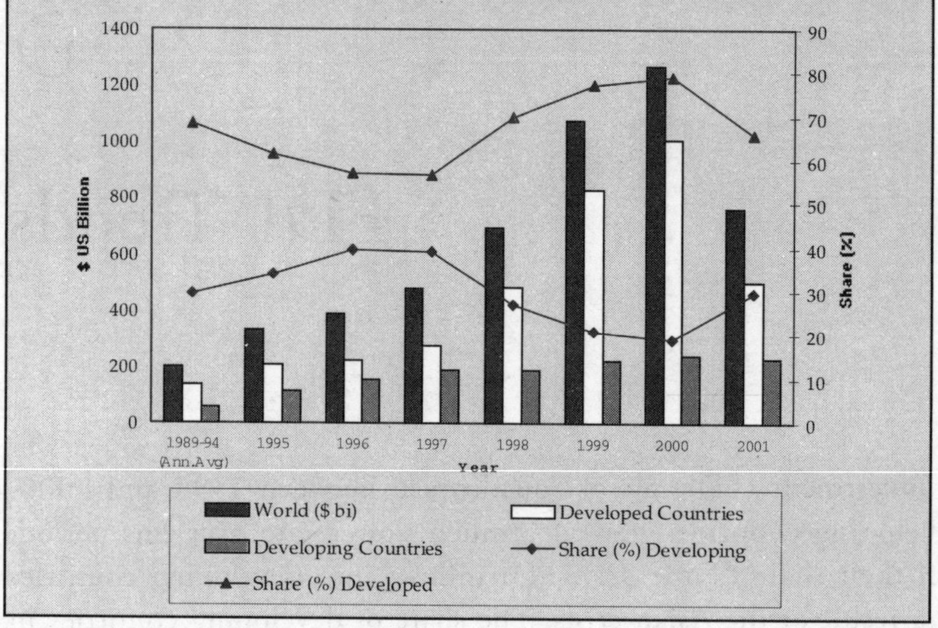

In 2000, China with 17 per cent had the highest share of developing country FDI followed by Brazil with 13.9 per cent of developing country FDI. The gap between the shares of these two countries narrowed during the nineties with Brazil gradually catching up with China, but has again widened in 2001. Though the share of Argentina, South Korea, Singapore, Malaysia and Taiwan is much lower than that of China and Brazil, it was, till 2000 two to five times that of India's measured inflow.[3] The most remarkable transformation has occurred in South Korea, whose share in developing country FDI inflows was identical to that of India in 1993, and which fell below that of India in 1994 and 1995, but was four times that of India's in 2000 (Figure 3.2). Because of the Asian crisis in 1997-98 and the effect of sanctions on investor's sentiment, India's share of developing country FDI fell at the end of the nineties. There has however been a significant improvement during 2001.

1. The Economist issue of June 29, 2002 has also acknowledged last year's record inflow of FDI as a promising feature.
2. The EIU report on 'World Investment Prospects 2002' projects an annual average FDI inflow of US $ 5.3 billion for India during 2002-06.
3. Please see section 3.3 for data comparability problems. There are also large differences in systems and approach, as summarised in appendix section 7.3.6.

TABLE – 3.2

FDI Inflows into Selected Countries

(Share of developing country total, per cent)

Host Region/ Economy	1989-94 (ann.avg)	1995	1996	1997	1998	1999	2000	2001
Developing Countries (in billion $)	59.6	113.3	152.5	187.4	188.4	222.0	240.2	225.0
Argentina	4.5	4.9	4.5	4.9	3.9	10.9	4.7	
Brazil	2.5	4.9	6.9	10.0	15.1	14.1	13.9	8.9
China	23.5	31.6	26.4	23.6	23.2	18.2	17.0	20.8
Indonesia	2.5	3.8	4.1	2.5	-0.2	-1.2	-1.9	
India	0.7	1.9	1.7	1.9	1.4	1.0	1.0	1.7*
Malaysia	6.2	5.1	4.8	3.5	1.4	1.6	2.3	
South Korea	1.5	1.6	1.5	1.5	2.9	4.8	4.2	
Singapore	8.1	7.8	6.8	6.9	3.3	3.2	2.7	
Thailand	3.2	1.8	1.5	1.9	2.7	1.6	1.0	
Taiwan	2.0	1.4	1.2	1.2	0.1	1.3	2.0	
Vietnam	1.0	2.0	1.6	1.5	1.2	0.9	0.9	

Source : World Investment Report 2001 & UNCTAD Press Release dated 21st Jan. 2002. Data for India may be under estimated for reasons given in subsequent section.

Note : *For 2001 India data is from RBI (FDI inflow in 2001-02 was $ 3904 million). Data in respect of other countries is not available.

India's measured FDI as a percentage of total Gross Domestic Product (GDP) is quite low in comparison to other competing countries (Table 3.3). India, the 12th largest country in the world in terms of GDP at current exchange rates is able to attract FDI equal only to 0.9 per cent of its GDP in 2001. In contrast FDI inflows into Vietnam were 6.8 per cent of its GDP in 2000. Even Malaysia, which has recently developed an image of being somewhat against the globalisation paradigm, receives FDI equal to 3.9 per cent of its GDP. Similarly

Figure 3.2: Selected Country FDI Inflows 1995-2001

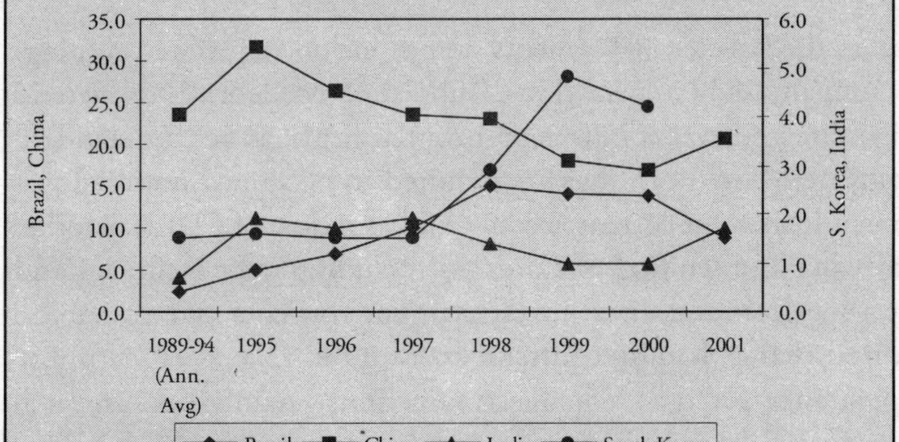

China attracts FDI equal to 3.8 per cent of its GDP. Thailand, which has a relatively low FDI-GDP ratio among the major developing country recipients of FDI, had a ratio four times that of India in 2000. This gap probably narrowed in 2001 and could narrow further in 2002 if the recent acceleration in growth of FDI into India can be sustained.

TABLE – 3.3

Ratio of FDI inflows to Gross Domestic Product

(per cent)

Developing Countries	1995	1996	1997	1998	1999	2000	2001
Argentina	2.0	2.5	3.1	2.4	8.5	3.9	
Brazil	0.8	1.4	2.3	3.6	5.9	5.7	
China	5.1	4.9	4.9	4.6	4.1	3.8	
Indonesia	2.2	2.7	2.2	-0.4	-1.9	-3.0	
India	0.6	0.7	0.9	0.6	0.5	0.5	0.9*
Malaysia	6.8	7.2	6.5	3.8	4.4	3.9	
S. Korea	0.4	0.4	0.6	1.7	2.6	2.2	
Singapore	10.5	11.4	13.7	7.6	8.6	7.0	
Thailand	1.2	1.3	2.4	4.6	3.0	2.0	
Vietnam	11.5	10.9	10.0	8.5	6.9	6.8	

Source : World Investment Report, 2001 and World Development Reports. Data for India may be underestimated for reasons given in next section.

Note : * India's GDP for 2001-02 at current prices was Rs.2068810 crore converted to US dollars using the exchange rate of 2001-02 at Rs.47.69. FDI inflow in 2001-02 was US $ 3904 million. Data for other countries not available for 2001.

3.3 Comparability of Data

India's FDI inflow estimates, in the Balance of Payments do not include reinvested earnings (by foreign companies), inter-company debt transactions (subordinated debt) and overseas commercial borrowings by foreign direct investors in foreign invested firms, as per the standard IMF definitions. Methodologically, reinvested earnings are required to be shown notionally as dividends paid out under investment income in current account and as inflow of FDI. The other capital, in turn, covers the borrowing and lending of funds — including debt securities and suppliers' credit — between direct investors and direct investment enterprises. From a technical point of view, it is well recognized that it is quite difficult to capture 'reinvested earnings' through the reporting arrangements for foreign exchange transactions, mainly because such transactions do not take place though it have to be imputed in the balance of payments statistics.

Direct investment, other capital transactions between direct investors and direct investment enterprises, however, pass through the banking channel. *There exists, however, the problem of identifying and isolating mutual borrowing and lending of funds among direct investors and direct investment enterprises.* Recognizing the above-mentioned constraints, greater reliance needs to be placed on collection of such data through direct investors' survey. The proper coverage of such transactions in India depends, therefore, upon the availability of information through the survey. **The data on inward FDI for India at present do not include reinvested earnings and 'other direct capital investment.'**

In this context, the National Statistical Commission recommended conducting periodical surveys on dividends and profits arising out of foreign direct investment and portfolio investment separately. In pursuance of the recommendation, a survey is being launched by the Reserve Bank of India to collect detailed information on FDI. Some estimate on reinvested earnings and other capital would be available from the survey and the data on inward FDI could be subsequently revised to include the data on reinvested earnings and other capital.

This issue has come into sharp focus because Dr. Guy Pfefferman, Chief Economist of the IFC estimated that India's actual FDI inflow might be between US$ 5 billion and US$ 8 billion during 2001.[4] The upper limit of US$ 8 billion is based on the assumption of a 40 per cent return on equity to foreign investors, which seems on the face of it to be somewhat high.[5] It should be remembered, however, that in contrast to several other countries in Asia, FDI inflows into India started over a half century ago. If the retained earnings from all these are cumulated, then the current returns on the stock of retained earnings would have to be added to the returns on measured FDI. Added together, these total returns would be high relative to the stock of measured FDI.

There is an additional problem of non-comparability when comparing the FDI flows of different countries with China, which also applies to China-India comparisons. According to Global Development Finance, 2002, round tripping amounts to nearly 50 per cent of total FDI inflows into China in 1999 and 2000. This would reduce China's real FDI share to about 9 per cent of developing country inflows and its adjusted FDI-GDP ratio to 1.8 per cent in 2000. Thus in 2000 the adjusted FDI-GDP ratio for China would be only double the adjusted FDI-GDP ratio for India.[6]

3.4 FDI in Privatisation

In recent years privatisation and dis-investment of public enterprises have become an important channel for the flow of FDI into many emerging economies (Appendix section 8.5).[7]

4. Presentation made by Mr Pfefferman at a seminar in Washington DC in April 2002.
5. Clarification given by the author in an email to the member-secretary of the committee.
6. Using the Pfefferman (2002) methodology
7. World Investment Report, 2000/2001, UNCTAD.

Brazil amongst all has been the most successful countries in using privatisation to attract FDI. The annual FDI inflow into Brazil through the privatisation process during the nineties has ranged between 1.5 per cent to 2 per cent of GDP. Of the over US$ 90 billion of privatisation proceeds garnered during this period, nearly 35 per cent of it was contributed by FDI. The sectors that were privatised include steel, petroleum, fertiliser, power, telecommunications, utilities, gas, banks, and ports. In other words, privatisation linked FDI has been primarily responsible for Brazil's quantum jump in FDI inflows. Similarly, a significant proportion of FDI in Argentina and Chile was also through route of privatisation of state owned companies.

Privatisation-related FDI transactions have been a key determinant of FDI inflows in Central and Eastern European countries as well. Poland, for example, has been one of the most aggressive in attracting FDI through the privatisation route. Over 2000 firms have been privatised between 1990-2000 involving US$ 7 billion. In 2000, purchase of shares of Telekomunikacja Polska (Poland) by France Telecom alone accounted for inflow of US$ 4 billion. Similar large FDI flows are also seen in Czech Republic and Hungary.

China has also embarked on an aggressive programme of converting departmental enterprises into corporations and privatising government companies. Between June 1999 to December 2001, China has raised over US$ 23 billion, mainly through the Initial Public Offering (IPO) route. The major transactions include China Mobile, China Unicom, China Petroleum and Chemical Corporation, Petro China and China Telecom. In November 2000, China Mobile (Hong Kong) acquired 7 mobile networks in the mainland, with a deal value of US$ 33 billion. As the deal was partly financed by capital raised through new shares issued to its parent company in the British Virgin Islands, there were FDI inflows of nearly US$ 23 billion into Hong Kong, China.

Given the slow start of disinvestment in India, there have been little or no foreign inflows into disinvestment. The small amount of foreign inflows has primarily been in the form of GDRs or ADRs. Over the past two years, the policy on 'strategic sale' has been clearly enunciated and implemented. This has begun to change the perception of potential FDI investors. Flows through this channel may be dependent on removal of sector specific barriers and public encouragement to FDI into privatisation. Even though this is a politically sensitive issue, from an economic viewpoint it would be reasonable to conclude that the disinvestment process has not resulted in additional foreign saving capital being injected into the country. This has not enabled India to secure one of the significant advantage of privatisation experienced in other countries.

3.5 Direction of FDI into India

Engineering, Services, Electronics and Electrical equipment and Computers were the main sectors receiving FDI in 2000-01 (Tables 3.5a and 3.5b). Domestic appliances, finance, food

& dairy products which were important sectors attracting FDI in the early nineties, have now seen a downtrend in the latter half of the nineties. Services and computer have seen an increasing trend in the latter half of the nineties. The inflow of FDI into computers increased from 6 per cent in 1999-00 to 16 per cent in 2000-01. On the whole there have been significant changes in the pattern and composition of FDI inflows with few clear trends over the decade as whole.

TABLE – 3.5A

Flow of Foreign Direct Investment into Different Sectors

(US $ million)

Sector/ Industry	1992 -93	1993 -94	1994 -95	1995 -96	1996 -97	1997 -98	1998 -99	1999 -00	2000 -01
Chemicals & Allied products	47	72	141	127	304	257	376	120	137
Engineering	70	33	132	252	730	580	428	326	273
Domestic Appliances	16	2	108	1	15	60			
Finance	4	42	98	270	217	148	185	20	40
Services	2	20	93	100	15	321	369	116	226
Electronics & Electrical Equipment	33	57	56	130	154	645	228	172	213
Food & Dairy Products	28	44	61	85	238	112	18	121	75
Computers	8	8	10	52	59	139	106	99	306
Pharmaceuticals	3	50	10	55	48	34	28	54	62
Others	69	76	162	347	278	660	262	553	578
Total	280	403	872	1419	2058	2956	2000	1581	1910

TABLE – 3.5B

Sectoral Distribution of Foreign Direct Investment

(As a percentage of total)

Sector/Industry	1992 -93	1993 -94	1994 -95	1995 -96	1996 -97	1997 -98	1998 -99	1999 -00	2000 -01
Chemicals & Allied products	17	18	16	9	15	9	19	8	7
Engineering	25	8	15	18	35	20	21	21	14
Domestic Appliances	6	1	12	0	1	2	0	0	0
Finance	1	10	11	19	11	5	9	1	2
Services	1	5	11	7	1	11	18	7	12
Electronics & Electrical Equipment	12	14	6	9	7	22	11	11	11
Food & Dairy Products	10	11	7	6	12	4	1	8	4
Computers	3	2	1	4	3	5	5	6	16
Pharmaceuticals	1	12	1	4	2	1	1	3	3
Others	25	19	19	24	14	22	13	35	30
Total	100	100	100	100	100	100	100	100	100

Source : RBI Annual Reports

4

Causes and Reasons for Low FDI

In this section we highlight some of the weakness and constraints on achieving higher FDI inflows into India. Not all are relevant to every originating country or every destination sector. Some factors are more relevant for first time investors with no previous experience of investment in India. The review presents broad generalisations based on the perceptions of potential foreign investors and independent consultants who interact closely with them. Some of the factors mentioned, may be based on past experience that is no longer valid because of recent improvements. Our objective is to extract a kernel of truth from these perceptions so as to help improve our policy and procedures even further.

4.1 Image and Attitude

Though economic reforms welcoming foreign capital were introduced in the nineties, it does not seem so far to be really evident in our overall attitude. There is a lingering perception abroad that foreign investors are still looked at with some suspicion. There is also a view that some unhappy episodes in the past have a multiplier effect by adversely affecting the business environment in India. Besides the "Made in India" label is not conceived by the world as synonymous with quality.

When a foreign investor considers making any new investment decision, *it goes through four stages in the decision making process and action cycle, namely,* **(a) screening, (b) planning, (c) implementing and (d) operating and expanding.**

The biggest barrier for India is at the first, screening stage itself in the action cycle. "Often India looses out at the screening stage itself" (BCG). This is primarily because we do not get across effectively to the decision-making "board room" levels of corporate entities where a final decision is taken. Our promotional effort is quite often of a general nature and not corporate specific. India is, moreover, a multi-cultural society and a large number of multi-national companies (MNC) do not understand the diversity and the multi-plural nature of the society and the different stakeholders in this country. Though in several cases, the foreign investor is discouraged even before he seriously considers a project, 220 of the Fortune 500 companies have some presence in India and several surveys (JBIC, Japan Exim bank, A T Kearney) show India as the most promising and profitable destination.

On the other hand China is viewed as 'more business oriented,' its decision- making is faster and has more FDI friendly policies (ATK 2001). Despite a very similar historical mistrust of foreigners and foreign investment arising from colonial experience, modern (post 1980 China) differs fundamentally from India. Its official attitude to FDI, reflected from the highest level of government (PM, President) to the lowest level of government bureaucracy (provinces) is one of consciously enticing FDI with a warm welcome. They recognise the multifaceted and mutual benefits arising from FDI.

All investments, foreign and domestic are made under the expectation of future profits. The economy benefits if economic policy fosters competition, creates a well functioning modern regulatory system and discourages 'artificial' monopolies created by the government through entry barriers. A recognition and understanding of these facts can result in a more positive attitude towards FDI.

4.2 Policy Framework

Most of the problems for investors arise because of domestic policy, rules and procedures and not the FDI policy per se or its rules and procedures. The FDI policy, which has a lot of positive features, is summarised first, before highlighting the domestic policy related difficulties that are commonly the focus of adverse comment by investors and intermediaries (Appendix section 8.3).

4.2.1 FDI Policy

India has one of the most transparent and liberal FDI regimes among the emerging and developing economies.[8] By FDI regime we mean those restrictions that apply to foreign nationals and entities but not to Indian nationals and Indian owned entities. The differential treatment is limited to a few entry rules, spelling out the proportion of equity that the foreign entrant can hold in an Indian (registered) company or business. There are a few banned sectors (like lotteries & gaming and legal services) and some sectors with limits on foreign equity proportion. The entry rules are clear and well defined and equity limits for foreign investment in selected sectors such as telecom quite explicit and well known.

8. See also appendix section 8.3.3.

Most of the manufacturing sectors have been for many years on the 100 per cent automatic route. Foreign equity is limited only in production of defence equipment (26 per cent), oil marketing (74 per cent) and government owned petroleum refineries (26 per cent). Most of the mining sectors are similarly on the 100 per cent automatic route, with foreign equity limits only on atomic minerals (74 per cent), coal & lignite (74 per cent),[9] exploration for oil (51 per cent to 74 per cent) and diamonds and precious stones (74 per cent). 100 per cent equity is also allowed in non-crop agro-allied sectors and crop agriculture under controlled conditions (e.g. hot houses).

In the case of infrastructure services, there is a clear dichotomy. While highways and roads, ports, inland waterways and transport, and urban infrastructure and courier services are on the 100 per cent automatic route, telecom (49 per cent), airports (74 per cent), civil aviation (40 per cent) and oil and gas pipelines (51 per cent) have foreign equity limits.[10] India also has a clear policy of FDI in services, with 100 per cent automatic entry into many services such as construction, townships/resorts, hotels, tourism, films, IT/ISP/email/voice mail, business services & consultancy, renting and leasing, VCFs and VCCs, medical/health, education, advertising and wholesale trade. The financial intermediation section has sectoral caps like banking (49 per cent), insurance (26 per cent), as do some services like professional services (51 per cent).

Subject to these foreign equity conditions a foreign company can set up a registered company in India and operate under the same laws, rules and regulations as any Indian owned company would. Unlike many countries including China, India extends National Treatment to foreign investors. There is absolutely no discrimination against foreign invested companies registered in India or in favour of domestic owned ones. There is however a minor restriction on those foreign entities who entered a particular sub-sector through a joint venture with an Indian partner. If they (i.e. the parent) want to set up another company in the same sector it must get a no-objection certificate from the joint-venture partner. This condition is explicit and transparent unlike many hidden conditions imposed by some other recipients of FDI. There are also a few prudential conditions on the sale of shares in unlisted companies and the above market price sale of shares in public companies.

4.2.2 Domestic Policy

The domestic policy framework affects all investment, whether the investor is Indian or foreign. To an extent, foreign companies or investors that have set up an Indian company or Joint Venture have become indigenised and thus can operate more or less competitively with other Indian company. They adjust themselves to the milieu. This is not, however, true of foreign direct investors who are coming into India for the first time. To the uninitiated the hurdles look daunting and the complexity somewhat perplexing.

9. No limit for captive use.
10. IT related investment has either 74 per cent limit or none (i.e. 100 per cent)

Among the policy problems that have been identified by surveys as acting as additional hurdles for FDI are laws, regulatory systems and Government monopolies that do not have contemporary relevance. Illustratively, the outdated Food Price Order (FPO) and Prevention of Food Adulteration Act are a major hurdle for FDI in food processing. The latter makes even a technical or minor violation subject to criminal liability. As a Task force had recommended some years ago, that we need to formulate a single integrated Food Act (including weights & measures). This should also make provision for a modern Food Regulatory system with a single integrated regulator. Based on the announcement in the last budget a Group of Ministers has been constituted to evolve a modern food law. The Essential Commodities Act adds to the difficulty of entering the food processing industry by making the procurement, storage and transport of agricultural produce subject to many vagaries and undermining the competitive advantage that India possesses. The Central government has recently taken steps to reduce the ambit of this act and eliminate controls on movement and storage of food grain. Initial steps have also been taken in the direction of putting this act into suspended state to be invoked only by a Central government notification to be applied only to well-specified emergency conditions like drought, floods and other natural disasters for a specific area and duration. Other simplification measures announced in the last budget were the amendment of the Milk and Milk products Control Order to remove restrictions on milk processing capacity, decanalisation of the export of agricultural commodities and phasing out of remaining export controls, expansion of futures and forward trading to cover all agricultural commodities and amendment to the Agriculture Produce Marketing Acts to enable farmers to sell directly to potential processors.

Similarly labour laws discourage the entry of green field FDI because of the fear that it would not be possible to downsize if and when there is a downturn in business. Labour laws, rules and procedures have led to a deterioration in the work culture and the comparative advantage that is even beginning to be recognised by responsible Trade Unions. Pursuant to the announcement in the 2001-02 budget that labour laws would be reformed, a Group of Ministers was set up to work out the modalities. The Labour Commission has in the meanwhile also submitted its report. The Group of Ministers will suggest specific changes in the laws for the approval of the Cabinet. SSI reservations further limit the possibility of entering labour intensive sectors for export. De-reservation of readymade garments during the year 2000 and de-reservation of fourteen other items related to leather goods, shoes and toys during 2001 is a welcome development. About 10 per cent of the items on the list of items reserved for the small-scale sector have been freed over the past few years. These two policy constraints are particularly relevant for ***export oriented FDI***. More flexible labour laws that improve work culture and enhance productivity and SSI de-reservations will help attract employment generating FDI inflows of the kind seen in South East Asia in the seventies and eighties and in China since the nineties.

The Urban Land Ceiling Acts and Rent Control Acts in States are a serious constraint on the entire real estate sector. This is another sector that has attracted large amounts of FDI in many countries including China. Like the labour-intensive industrial sectors it can also generate a large volume of productive employment. These Acts need to be repealed if a construction boom is to be initiated that would reverse the decline in overall investment, attract FDI, generate employment and make rental accommodation available to the poor. The Centre has already repealed the Urban Land Ceiling Act but each State has to issue a notification to repeal the Act in that State. Rent Control is a State subject and each State would have to reform its Rent control Act. The Central government has set up an Urban Reform Facility to provide funds to States that repeal the State Land Ceiling Act, reform the Rent Control Act and carry out other urban reforms.

Weak credibility of regulatory systems and multiple and conflicting roles of agencies and government has an adverse impact on new FDI investors, which is greater than on domestic investors. All monopolists have a strong self-interest in preventing new entrants who can put competitive pressure. In the past, government monopoly in infrastructure sectors has slowed down policy reform. FDI was discouraged by the fear that pressure exerted by government monopolies through their parent departments would bias the regulatory system against new private competitors. As regulatory systems and procedures move up the learning curve, initial problems stemming from lack of regulatory knowledge/experience in sectors such as Telecom have been gradually overcome. Similarly, in the past, strategy and implementation problems connected with disinvestment created great uncertainty and increased policy/regulatory risk, resulting in a lack of interest of FDI investors in bidding for these companies. With a much clearer strategy and effective implementation over the past year and a half, there should be better inflow on this account.

According to some consultants, in the banking sector, controls on activity dampen FDI inflows. It is alleged that persistent fears of impending "fiscal crisis" is another constraint, and that a well articulated strategy for medium term fiscal consolidations would address these concerns. The absence of product patents in the chemicals sector has reduced inflows into the drugs and pharmaceuticals sector.

Though the foreign trade and tariff regime for Special Export Zones (SEZs) approximates a genuine free trade zone, the other elements of the policy framework and procedures remain virtually the same as in the Domestic Tariff Area. The SEZs are therefore still not fully on par with the Export Zones of China with respect to Labour Intensive production (Appendix section 8.4).

4.3 Procedures

According to Boston Consulting Group, investors find it frustrating to navigate through the tangles of bureaucratic controls and procedures.[11] McKinsey (2001) found that, the time taken for application/bidding/approval of FDI projects was too long. Multiple approvals, excessive time taken (2-3 years) such as in food processing and long lead times of up to six months for licenses for duty free exports, lead to "loss of investors' confidence despite promises of a considerable market size."

Bureaucracy and red tape topped the list of investor concerns as they were cited by 39 per cent of respondents in the A T Kearney survey. Of the three stages of a project, namely general approval (e.g. FDI, investment licence for items subject to licence), clearance (project specific approvals e.g. environmental clearance for specific location and product) and implementation, the second was the most oppressive.[12] Three-fourth of the respondents in the survey indicated that (post-approval) *clearances connected with investment* were the most affected by India's red tape. According to a CII study, *a typical power project requires 43 Central Government clearances and 57 State Government level (including the local administration) clearances.* Similarly, the number of clearances for a typical mining project are 37 at the Central Government level and 47 at the State Government level. Though the number of approvals/ clearances may not always be much lower in the OECD countries such as the USA and Japan the regulatory process is transparent with clear documentation requirements and decision rules based largely on self-certification, and generally implemented through the legal profession.[13]

The Government has set up an inter-ministerial Committee to examine the existing procedures for investment approvals and implementation of projects and suggest measures to simplify and expedite the process for both public and private investment. The Committee, which was set up in September 2002, has submitted Part I of its report (dealing with Public sector projects) to the Government, which is under examination. A sub-Group of the Committee is specifically looking into simplification of procedures relating to private investment.

The respondents of the ATK survey also indicated that the divide between Central and State governments in the treatment of foreign investors could undermine the FDI promotion efforts of the Central Government. The FICCI (2001) study similarly cites centre-state duality as creating difficulties at both the approval and project implementation stages. These studies find that the bureaucracy in general is quite unhelpful in extending infra-structural facilities to any project that is being set up. This *leads to time and cost overruns.* At an operational level, multiple returns have to be filed every month.

One effect of these bureaucratic delays is the low levels of realization of FDI inflows vis-à-vis the proposals cleared (CII). Although the realization rate has improved to 45 per cent in 2000-

11. See also appendix section 8.3.1 and 8.3.2.
12. The definition of approval and clearance are not standardised. Our usage is consistent with CII's, while that of A T Kearny appears to be the opposite/inverse.
13. The Govindarajan committee is dealing comprehensively with these issues.

01 compared to 21 per cent in 1997, it remains a matter of concern. The precise reason for the low levels of realization is *the post approval procedures,* which has in the past played havoc with project implementation.

4.3.1 FIPB

It should be noted, that the delays mentioned by foreign investors are not at the stage of FDI approval per se i.e. at the entry point whether through RBI automatic route or FIPB approval.[14] The FIPB considers application on the basis of notified guidelines and disposes them within a 6-8 week timeframe, as has been laid down by the Cabinet. The entire process of FIPB applications, starting from their registration through to listing on FIPB agenda and their final disposal and despatch on official communication is placed on the website, which adds to the transparency of decision-making and enhances investor confidence. Similarly, the underlying advisory support in the form of online chat facility and dedicated e-mail facility for existing and prospective investors has created an investor friendly image. A FICCI Study on, "Impediments to Investment" (January 2002) has acknowledged that the Central level FIPB clearances have been successfully streamlined. The FIPB approval system has also been rated as world class by independent surveys conducted by CII and JICA.

The FIIA framework has also been strengthened recently by adoption of a six-point strategy. This includes close interaction with companies at both operational and board room level, follow up with administrative ministries, State Governments and other concerned agencies and sector specific approach in resolving investment related problems. The major implementation problems are encountered at the state level, as project implementation takes place at the state level. FICCI in its study on "Impediments to Investment" has observed that *the Regional meetings for foreign investors under the FIIA chaired by the Industry Secretary are now turning out to be problem-solving platforms.*

4.4 Quality of Infrastructure

Poor infrastructure affects the productivity of the economy as a whole and hence its GDP/ per capita GDP.[15] It also reduces the comparative advantage of industries that are more intensive in the use of such infrastructure. In the context of FDI, poor infrastructure has a greater effect on export production than on production for the domestic market. FDI directed at the domestic market suffers the same handicap and additional costs as domestic manufacturers that are competing for the domestic market. Inadequate and poor quality roads, railroads and ports, however raise export costs vis-a-vis global competitors having better quality and lower cost

14. See also appendix section 8.3.4.
15. In market determined exchange rate, this is reflected in an exchange rate that is more depreciated than it would be if infrastructure was efficient.

infrastructure.[16] As a foreign direct investor planning to set up an export base in developing/emerging economies has the option of choosing between India and other locations with better infrastructure, India is handicapped in attracting export oriented FDI.

Poor infrastructure is found to be the most important constraint for construction and engineering industries. "Law, rules, regulations relating to infrastructure are sometimes missing or unclear e.g. LNG and the power sector is beset with multiple problems such as State monopoly, bankruptcy and weak regulators" (McKinsey 2001).

4.5 State Obstacles

Taxes levied on transportation of goods from State to State (such as octroi and entry tax) adversely impact the economic environment for export production. Such taxes impose both cost and time delays on movement of inputs used in production of export products as well as in transport of the latter to the ports. Differential sale and excise taxes (States and Centre) on small and large companies are found to be a deterrent to FDI in sectors such as textiles (McKinsey 2001). Investments that could raise the productivity and quality of textiles and thus make them competitive in global markets remain unprofitable because they cannot overcome the tax advantage given to small producers in the domestic market.

Globally the service sector received 43 per cent of total investment in emerging markets in 1997 (ATK 2001). As this is a State subject, the States have to take the lead in simplifying and modernising the policy and rules relating to this sector.

At the local level (sub-state) issues pertaining to land acquisition, land use change, power connection, building plan approval are sources of project implementation delay. The State level issues are also being considered by the Govindarajan committee with a view to seeing how they can be alleviated.

4.6 Legal Delays

Though India's Anglo Saxon legal system as codified is considered by many legal experts to be superior to that of many other emerging economies it is often found in practice to be an obstacle to investment. One of the reasons for the inordinate delay is the interlocutory procedures that characterise judicial procedures. As a result the "Rule of law," which has often been cited as one of the attractive features of the Indian economy for foreign investors, is found to be a significant positive factor by only 3 per cent for FDI in India. In contrast, 26 per cent of all those surveyed by ATK (2001) cited this as an important factor in their global investment decisions.

16. These costs have been quantified by the CII-World Bank study of Investment environment in India and its comparison with similar World Bank studies on China and other countries.

5

Recommendations

5.1 Regulatory Reforms

The proposed regulatory reforms are stand-alone reforms and therefore *neither* mutually exclusive *nor* sequential in nature.

5.1.1 Foreign Investment Law

At present, the entire FDI policy and procedures, as notified by the Government from time to time, are duly incorporated under FEMA regulations. FEMA also covers all issues related to foreign exchange management such as issue/valuation/transfer of shares, divestment of original investment, foreign technology collaboration payments, repatriation of profits, acquisition and disposal of immovable property etc. by foreigners.

Brazil is in a similar position to us in that it does not have a separate Foreign Investment law. Malaysia's Industrial Co-ordination Act (1975) has foreign investment and technology transfer policy as an integral element. This act is supplemented by the Malaysian Industrial Development Authority Act (MIDA), which provides an institutional and legal framework for a single point facilitation of FDI into Malaysia. China, Vietnam and South Korea have separate laws dealing with foreign investment. With a closed almost anti-FDI stance during the early decades of socialism, China's (1979) and Vietnam's (1987) acts signalled an "open door" policy with guarantee of legal protection for foreign investment. In contrast South Korea's post Asian crisis legislation lays emphasis on promotion of FDI. Korea's Foreign Investment Promotion Act (1998) has a provision for the **Office of Investment Ombudsman** to redress grievances and solve problems of foreign investors.

Consideration may be given to the enactment of a foreign investment promotion law. This law would be administered by the Department of Industrial Policy and Promotion as against the present administration of the Foreign Exchange Management Act (FEMA) by the Directorate of Enforcement. Even optically the activity of encouraging FDI is a promotional one and not a regulatory one. A separate investment promotion law would meet this objective and signal a change in attitude from regulation to promotion. A legal group should be constituted to draft a new law that would have as its objectives, (i) the promotion of FDI and (ii) National treatment for FDI. This law could also deal with issues such as double taxation, making a provision for preferential treatment of FDI, where this is considered to be in the national/public interest and help overcome obstacles arising from hurdles created at the State level for infrastructure sectors that are on the Central list. It has to be kept in mind, however that the Indian system is much more democratic in practice and has stronger rights for States. The Korean Investment Promotion Act supplemented by the Malaysian MIDA Act could be used as a model for framing suitable legislation.

5.1.2 State Laws on Infrastructure

Infrastructure investment and exports can be key drivers of productivity change and economic growth. Both domestic private and foreign direct investment can play an important role in these areas, but FDI can potentially play a more than proportionate role because of the special features of these sectors. Critical infrastructure investments are capital intensive. Easier access of foreign investors to capital resources and their global expertise can expedite investment, if the policy framework and regulatory structures are appropriate. Similarly the knowledge, experience and connectivity of foreign companies to global markets give them an advantage in export markets for manufactured goods.

We therefore recommend that the States consider enacting a special Investment Law covering infrastructure investment. This law would apply to both domestic and foreign investment. The Andhra Pradesh Infrastructure Act provides a useful template on which other States' laws could be based (Copy annexed).[17]

This law would cover issues connected to investment in and production of infrastructure services. The objective of this law would be to integrate to the extent feasible, the many State laws, rules and regulations applicable to these critical sectors. It could thus potentially cover environmental clearances, industrial relations, worker health and safety etc. It could also specify special labour laws, rules and procedures for investment in infrastructure and production/supply of infrastructure services. It would have simplified rules and regulations and would specify and enforce time limits on all relevant clearances. A statutory body should be defined and set up

17. The experience of the Gujarat government in attracting private investment/FDI in ports and other infrastructure could also be drawn upon.

under the Act, whose primary objective would be to increase and speed up private investment in these sectors. This body could also have some members from the private sector.

5.2 Institutional Changes

5.2.1 Industry Department

Within the government, the Department of Industrial Policy and Promotion (DIPP) is responsible for foreign investment, with the Secretary (DIPP) chairing the Foreign Investment Promotion Board (FIPB), the nodal agency for FDI. The Foreign Investment Implementation Authority (FIIA), designed to assist foreign direct investors with respect to post-approval operational problems is also serviced by the Secretariat for Industrial Assistance (SIA) in the DIPP (Appendix section 8.3.4). There is a need to strengthen both the FIPB and the FIIA so as to increase their effectiveness in removing procedural bottlenecks and reducing bureaucratic red tape.

The FIPB could be empowered to give initial Central government level registration and approvals where possible, such as company incorporation, DGFT registration, customs and excise registration, income tax registration etc. The objective would be to speed up the process of getting regulatory and administrative approvals, so that it could be more effective in promoting FDI. A composite form containing such entry-level Central registration/approvals should be devised, with a time bound referral system to speed up company incorporation, DGFT registration, customs and excise registration, income tax registration etc., within the FIPB clearance system.[18]

The Transaction of Business rules should be modified to empower the Foreign Investment Implementation Authority (FIIA) so as to enable it fix the time frame for investment related approvals both at the State and Central levels. In regard to Central level approvals, FIIA would be empowered to bring persistent delays to the attention of the Cabinet Committee on Foreign Investment so that it can issue appropriate directions to the administrative ministries if they fail to respond conclusively within the prescribed time limit.[19]

With greater automaticity in foreign direct investment, fewer and fewer cases require FIPB approval and its regulatory functions are getting reduced. The emphasis henceforth would be increasingly on the promotional aspects. There is, nonetheless, a need for a sound database. An FDI registration system can be useful in creating the necessary database for tracking speedy implementation of FDI projects. This arrangement would be in lieu of the Industrial Entrepreneurs Memorandum (IEM) registration, which is not sufficiently comprehensive. It must be ensured

18. The Govindarajan Committee in its first report has analysed the regulatory hassles in public projects.

19. If, as recommended by the Govindarajan committee, an Industrial Investment Facilitation Board is set up to cover all investment, public and private, above some value (e.g. Rs. 100 crore), then the ambit of FIIA may have to be restricted to avoid overlap.

however that such a registration system does not in future become an instrument for control or interference in the functioning of FDI and is used merely for acceleration of approved FDI.

An exercise using PERT/CPM chart techniques has been carried out to identify clearance process bottlenecks. This covers both the Centre and States. After mapping the delays, procedures for reducing delays are also being worked out by the Govindarajan Committee.

5.2.2 Planning and FDI Sector Targets

If FDI flows of over US$ 8 billion is to be attained over the next five years all wings of government have to be made responsible and accountable for increasing private investment in general and FDI in particular. Sector wise FDI targets could be set and sector ministries made responsible for achieving these targets. An illustrative/indicative list of sector wise FDI targets is given in Table 5.2.2. These illustrative/indicative sector targets have been worked out taking into consideration the target of US$ 7-8 billion projected for the first two years of the Tenth Five Year Plan. The sectoral estimations include *green field investments* and *mergers and acquisitions,* but do not include privatisation targets. Aggregate illustrative target for the latter is given separately. These targets should be refined in discussions between the Planning Commission, the sector departments, Department of Industrial Policy and Promotion, Ministry of Finance, and the Ministry of External Affairs.

These sectoral targets are lower than those indicated by McKinsey & Company in their report titled "Achieving a quantum leap in India's FDI."

TABLE – 5.2.2

Illustrative/Indicative Sectoral Annual FDI Targets

	Sector	FDI Target (US $ billion)
1.	Telecom	2.5
2.	Power	1.2
3.	Financial Services	0.8
4.	LNG & Oil exploration	1.0
5.	Software & IT enabled services	1.0
6.	Food & beverage	0.4
7.	Transportation	0.4
8.	Textiles	0.3
9.	Ports	0.3
10.	Chemicals & Petrochemicals	0.2
11.	Hotels & Tourism	0.2

Contd...

Contd...

12.	Real Estate	0.2
13.	Roads	0.2
14.	Civil Aviation	0.2
15.	Disinvestment	0.5
	Total	8.9

5.2.3 Fund for Assistance to States

An investment facilitation fund can be set up to provide assistance to those States who need assistance in modifying policies and procedures for promoting foreign and domestic investment. This could have two components: technical assistance and financial assistance. The latter could be made contingent on State specific reforms.

The States could use these funds to prepare project reports for a shelf of projects in which FDI is desired to speed up the growth of the State. They could also use these funds to market these projects to foreign investors. The project could be funded through suitable Plan Allocation on the pattern of the International Centre for Advancement of Manufacturing Technology (ICAMT) project, which has been jointly set up by UNIDO and GOI. The Project for investment promotion could build capacity of State Investment Promotion agencies (IPAs), create a dynamic network of IPAs and promote sectoral investment opportunities. The project deliverables could be the development of tools for IPAs, skill enhancement, preparation of marketing plans, etc.

The investment facilitation fund should have an effective implementation agency to help States in capacity building in the areas of investment promotion and facilitation like construction of investment road maps, investment tracking system, on mirroring as closely as possible a single-window facility. A task force/project approach is considered the most suitable for this purpose. The National Leather Development Programme (NLDP), jointly funded by UNDP and GOI and the Indian Leather Development Programme (ILDP) funded by GOI could serve as models. The NLDP and ILDP are implemented through UNDP with clearly laid down milestones supported by a robust monitoring and evaluation mechanism. They are among the better-implemented programmes in the country. UNIDO, with a strong network of Investment and Technology Promotion Offices and expertise in investment and technology promotion and the Foreign Investment Advisory Services (FIAS), a body set up by the World Bank and IFC are potential implementation agents.

5.2.4 Non-governmental Facilitation Services

Some industry associations such as CII are already taking steps to help foreign direct investors in dealing with unfamiliar Indian procedures. This effort needs to be supported and expanded. A non-governmental Society or Council should be set up by industry associations with the help and encouragement of the government (DIPP), for assisting first time foreign investors. This organisation would operate on a non-profit basis and supply information, approval and clearance services to FDI investors. These could range from giving advice and information to a comprehensive service, which obtains all clearances and approvals for the FDI investor. For instance, first time FDI investors also find it difficult to find genuine and sincere joint venture partners. This society would facilitate the search for joint venture partners. This society/council could have representatives from industry associations, Multinational & other companies.

5.3 Raising FDI Sectoral CAPS

Given the imperative of attracting FDI for increasing India's GDP growth rate, there should be a presumption in favour of permitting FDI. Accordingly, entry barriers to FDI (i.e. over and above those applying to private investment generally) in any industry must be explicitly justified. The arguments that are used for imposition of caps and bans are analysed to see which may be justified.

5.3.1 National Security

As a general proposition all governments prefer vital defence industries to be controlled by their own resident nationals. There are however two dimensions of this issue that need to be considered in the Indian context. One is the boundary of the defence industry. There is absolutely no need to put equity restrictions on the production of civilian goods used by the defence forces. More importantly we need to distinguish between pure defence/security equipment such as weapons platforms and dual use equipment and parts that are also used in the production of civilian goods. A narrow boundary would imply that such dual use goods are treated as civilian and freed from FDI equity limits, while a broad boundary would imply the opposite. In any case FDI equity limits should in general be much more liberal for dual use items than for pure defence equipment.

The second dimension that is important in determining FDI equity limits is the domestic production versus import decision. Most discussion of FDI limits is carried out on the presumption that the item will be produced in India no matter what and the only choice is the level of FDI equity or management control. The reality is that considerable defence equipment is imported, more often than not from privately owned companies. In this situation the choice is much more likely to be between FDI with high level of foreign equity and management control and continued imports. The former would in most cases be much more preferable than the latter. Thus import substitution in defence industry should be allowed with much greater level of foreign equity.

The third dimension relates to bans imposed by developed countries on the import of defence and dual use goods and strategic technology. If unlimited equity share and tax benefits can help attract such technology into India, then the nation can benefit tremendously in the long run by achieving greater domestic control and self sufficiency.

5.3.2 Culture and Media

We should have no objection in principle to publications on culture, society and entertainment being published and sold in India as long as this is not at the expense of Indian culture, social norms and practices. One touchstone for deciding on foreign equity could be a criterion of true cultural globalisation. In other words globalisation of culture must be a two way street, with the rest of the World having the same access to Indian culture as we do to theirs. Globalisation of media cannot merely mean that all the existing cultural (e.g. soap operas) and nationalistic (e.g. war news) content created in democratic USA, UK and other English speaking countries is merely transferred to India. Globalisation must also mean that the cultural and nationalistic content created by one-sixth of the humanity living in democratic India is also in due course brought to a global audience. Our experience with the opening of TV media demonstrates the strength of Indian culture in that most foreign companies have been forced by the market to increase content based on Indian cultural and entertainment traditions and reduce transplanted foreign culture sensitive programs.

Some element of restriction can also be applied to foreign entrants in the field of current affairs and news programs. Reporting of international affairs is strongly influenced by nationality, as demonstrated by reporting of the war in Afghanistan and related issues of Pakistani involvement in terrorism in the South Asian region. Editorial control, in the sense of control over editorial policy and content must vest with Indian nationals. The business managers and those who control commercial decision can, however, be foreigners. Over time a more liberal policy that focuses on controlling dominance in terms of share of the market for news and current affairs is desirable. Thus FDI equity limits in terms of individual companies in this field could eventually be replaced by limits to the aggregate market share (25 per cent - 49 per cent) that can accrue to foreign controlled news/current affair companies taken together.

5.3.3 Natural Monopolies

Natural monopolies arise in the case of some non-tradable infrastructure sectors. These sectors or natural monopoly segments need to be regulated by independent regulators whether they are government or private, domestic or foreign owned. Efficient and effective regulation requires professional skills and knowledge. Independent and autonomous regulatory systems must be built so that the public benefits rather than the owners and/or managers of such 'natural monopolies.' It can be argued that when such expertise does not exist in the regulatory system it may be better for monopoly profits to accrue to resident nationals than to foreigners. Though this argument has some validity in the short term it is a defeatist approach in the long term. Domestic monopolists are more likely to succeed in distorting the regulatory process in their favour ('regulatory capture') than foreign monopolists, because of their more intimate knowledge of and association with domestic political processes. Any such restrictions must therefore be temporary with continuous efforts made to improve regulatory structures and skills.

We have adopted different approaches in various sectors. The power sector was opened early to 100 per cent foreign equity, followed thereafter by roads and ports. In telecom where the natural monopoly elements have virtually been eliminated by technological developments, the 49 per cent foreign equity limit has remained unchanged. The initial reasons for caution do not appear to be valid any more and the time has come for a more liberal approach. It is even more difficult to find significant 'natural monopoly' elements in civil aviation so that this argument cannot be used for justifying foreign equity or ownership restrictions in this sector.

5.3.4 Monopoly Power

In the case of tradable goods competition arises not just from domestic production but also from imports. A limited number of domestic producers need not denote monopoly power.[20] Modern competition law emphasises control of the abuse of monopoly power rather than focussing on the number of producers in a narrowly defined sub-sector. FDI can in fact enhance domestic competition if a global player sets up a green field project thus expanding the number of domestic producer of the good. There can, however, be a genuine concern if a foreign producer with very high global share tries to acquire an existing domestic producer from among a few remaining domestic producers. This is a potential problem that can and should be dealt with under the proposed competition law and does not require a cap on foreign equity holding.

5.3.5 Natural Resources

The ownership of natural resources such as the electro magnetic spectrum and sites for dams, harbours, vests in the people and their government. The resource rent is defined as the difference between market price and the efficient costs of exploitation of the particular resource at a particular time and place. The resource rent depends on scarcity of the resource and its quality. Resource rent tax systems and auctioning procedures have been designed to extract the highest proportion of such resource rent to the government. If these are effective there is no

20. This generally arises from high capital requirements for reaching minimum efficient scale or high marketing costs in building brand recognition.

reason to discriminate between FDI and domestic investment in production/use of such resources and consequently to put FDI limits on the former.[21]

The situation is somewhat different with respect to internationally created sovereign rights such as those created by IATA for international civil aviation. These artificially created rents accrue to the government and would be enhanced if they are fully exploited. Rent accrual would be enhanced if Air India was privatised without limits on foreign equity. However these rights vest in the sovereign and can only be assigned to 'National carriers' and majority ownership must remain with Indian nationals if these rights are to remain valid. Thus in this case foreign equity limits in Air India are justified as long as the IATA agreement is not modified and the old rules continue to remain.

5.3.6 Transition Costs

An important reason for encouraging FDI is the productivity gains that can accrue. But the flip side of this coin is the short-term transition costs that it imposes on existing less productive competitors. For instant FDI in food retailing (entry of food department store chain) would lead to more efficient supply chain management systems that can reduce the large gap between the price received by farmers and that paid by consumers.[22] It would thus benefit both farmers and consumers besides creating profitable avenues for FDI. But in the short term, traders and intermediaries in direct competition with these new entrants would suffer a loss in income. Over time the productivity gains would generate much more income and employment opportunities, even for these intermediaries, by stimulating agricultural growth and consumer demand. Similar opportunity and difficulties arise in the case of FDI in the organised retail sector (general department stores).[23]

The classical economic solution to this problem is to compensate the losers through direct budgetary assistance. The political economy, however, makes this somewhat difficult. A gradual approach has therefore to be adopted. This can consist either of first allowing a low level of foreign equity and then raising it gradually over time or of controlling/rationing the number of entrants so that they initially supply only a small proportion of the market (say the incremental demand).[24]

---

21. The national pool of human genes as well as the non-human gene pool is also a sovereign resource that can in principle have resource rents. The potential resource rents inherent in this resource needs to be estimated and accounted for in the national policy on bio-resources and their use.
22. This was shown by a McKinsey study on Food processing/retailing in several countries including India.
23. A recent McKinsey study shows that growth of productivity in the retail sector was the second most important source of the outstanding productivity growth in the US economy during the nineties.
24. A roll out plan to develop a domestic supply chain and train Indians in all aspects of supply chain management could be used to rank potential entrants.

5.3.7 Recommendations

Many of the remaining entry conditions had greater justification at the time they were imposed. With a much stronger and more competitive economy many of these can be removed. This will eliminate minor irritants that are sometimes blown out of proportion by interested parties to the detriment of the national interest. The committees' recommendations on the existing entry barriers to FDI are summarised in Table 5.3.7a.

TABLE – 5.3.7A

Proposed Changes in Sectoral Limits on FDI

S.No	Sector	Equity Limits		Entry Route		Change in Conditions
		Existing (1)	Proposed (2)	Existing (3)	Proposed (4)	(5)
I.	**Manufacturing**					
I.1	Drugs (recombinant DNA.)	100%	100%	FIPB	Automatic	
I.2	Petroleum Refining-PSUs	26%	100%	FIPB	Automatic	
I.3	Oil marketing	74%	100%	FIPB	Automatic	
I.4	SSI	24%	49%	Automatic	Automatic	export 50%->0%
II.	**Mining & Quarrying**					
II.1	Diamond, precious stones	74%	100%	Automatic	Automatic	
II.2.1	Petro Explore: small field,bid	100%	No change	FIPB	Automatic	
II.2.2	Petro Explore:Un incorp JV	60%	100%	FIPB	Automatic	
II.2.3	Petro Explore:Incorp JV	51%	100%	FIPB	Automatic	
II.3.1	Coal & Lignite	50%	100%	Automatic	Automatic	
	Power user	100%		FIPB	Automatic	
	Other user	74%		FIPB	Automatic	
II.3.2	Coal Washery	50%	100%	Automatic	Automatic	
		100%		FIPB	Automatic	
IV.	**Infrastructure Services**					
IV.1	Airports	74%	100%	Automatic	Automatic	
		100%		FIPB	Automatic	
IV.2	Civil Aviation	40%	49%	FIPB	Automatic	Incld. foreign airlines
IV.3	Telecom					
IV.3.1	Basic & Mobile	49%	74%	FIPB	No change	
IV.3.2	Total Bandwidth	74%	100%	FIPB	Automatic	
IV.3.3	Gateway	74%	100%	FIPB	Automatic	

Contd...

		(1)	(2)	(3)	(4)	(5)
IV.4	Pipeline:Oil & Gas	51%	100%	FIPB	Automatic	
V.	**Financial Services**					
V.1	Banking (private)	49%	100%	Automatic	No change	
V.3	Investing companies	49%	100%	FIPB	Automatic	
VI.	**Knowledge services**					
VI.1	Information Tech					
VI.1.1	ISP	100%	No change	FIPB	Automatic	
VI.1.2	Email, Voice mail	100%	No change	FIPB	Automatic	
VI.1.3	Radio Paging	74%	100%	FIPB	Automatic	
VI.2	Broadcasting-DTH,KU	20%	49%	FIPB	No change	Remove sub-limits (FDI, FII)
VI.2.1	Up linking	49%	No change	FIPB	No change	
VII.	**Other Services**					
VII.1	Advertising	74%	100%	Automatic	No change	
VII.2	Trading (export, SSI.)	51%	100%	Automatic		
		100%		FIPB	Automatic	
VII.3	Courier service	100%	No change	FIPB	Automatic	
VIII.	**Currently Banned Sectors**					
1.	Plantations (other)	0%	49%		FIPB	
2.	Real estate:					
2.1	Complexes (all categories)	0%	100%		Automatic	
2.2	Individual house/blding/shed	0%	100%		FIPB	

5.3.7.1 Manufacturing

The foreign equity limits on production of drugs using recombinant DNA technology or specific cell/tissue targeted formulations was recently raised from 74 per cent to 100 per cent. It, however, remains on the FIPB route. As all such processes are regulated by the biotechnology regulator (for both domestic and foreign investors) FIPB merely acts a redundant layer. We recommend a shift of this item to the automatic route.

Though 100 per cent FDI is allowed in private petroleum refineries, FDI in public sector refineries is restricted to 26 per cent. The public sector refineries are under the control of government appointed boards. Government as owner has the right to decide how much if any of its shares it wants to sell to a domestic or foreign investor. Further, as long as these refineries remain in the public sector government either has management control (50.1 per cent) or the right to veto any fundamental changes (25.1 per cent equity).[25] It can therefore either control

25. It can even have management control with 25 per cent share.

or directly supervise any FDI investor. When it has sold its last 25 per cent share the company becomes a private company and 100 per cent FDI is already allowed in this case. There is therefore no need for any equity limit and this should be raised to 100 per cent and put on the automatic route.

With a virtual monopoly of oil marketing currently in the public sector, with several Indian private players on the verge of entering this sector entry of foreign players will enhance competition. The power of Indians to block special resolutions serves no useful purpose and the FDI limit of 74 per cent can be raised to 100 per cent (automatic). The petroleum regulatory bill will in any case allow the regulator to give directions to all oil companies in the event of war and natural disaster.

With these three changes the entire manufacturing sector, except defence, will be on the 100 per cent automatic route.

Indian companies are currently prohibited to have more than 24 per cent equity in small-scale units (SSI).[26] The same limits are applicable to foreign direct investors (i.e. this is not strictly an FDI policy issue). These limits reduce the ability of SSI to raise equity capital. In a situation in which every expert and every shade of political opinions supports a greater flow of funds to the SSIs, the equity limits are illogical. If a small-scale enterprise wants to expand by offering equity to FDI investors or domestic companies, it should be free to do so. This will not only ease the financing constraint but promote backward and forward linkages with medium-large (domestic and foreign) industry. Such synergy is essential for healthy growth of both sectors and for enhancing industrial efficiency and competitive strength. We therefore recommend raising the equity limit to 49 per cent and placed on automatic route.[27]

5.3.7.2 Mining

There is currently an equity cap of 74 per cent on exploration for diamonds and precious stones. As the rights to mine any mineral vests with the government, no individual or company, domestic or foreign can extract any mineral from the ground without the explicit permission of the government. The government specifies various terms and conditions in these contracts (including resource rent or royalty) and the process is therefore fully under the control of the government. Nothing is gained from restricting foreign equity and the limit should be raised to 100 per cent.

For similar reasons the current restrictions on equity (74 per cent) in coal and lignite mining for non-power use should be removed and 100 per cent equity automatically allowed in coal mining. It may also be noted that restrictions under the Coal Nationalisation Act apply

26. Higher equity proportion is permitted if 50 per cent of output is exported.

27. Higher limits can also be permitted through the FIPB route in the case of committed exports.

to both foreign and domestic investors. Foreign investment in coal washeries, which is a processing activity, should also be put on the automatic route.

Foreign equity in petroleum exploration is automatically allowed up to 50 per cent but higher limits of 51 per cent, 60 per cent and 100 per cent are allowed through the FIPB route for incorporated joint ventures, unincorporated joint ventures and small fields given through the competitive bidding route. The economics of natural resources demonstrates clearly that the larger the number of companies interested in a particular field, the higher the share of rent appropriated by the government. If even one or two companies drop out of the race because of lower equity ceilings, the country looses and the explorer benefits. We therefore recommend that 100 per cent foreign equity on the automatic route be allowed for all petroleum exploration. As in any other exploration/mining contract the government is a contracting party and has direct say in the terms and conditions of the exploration.

In the case of atomic minerals, 74 per cent foreign equity is allowed through FIPB and even 100 per cent can be permitted if the Atomic Energy Commission approves. The entire FIPB process focuses on the national security and proliferation issues that are fully covered by the Atomic Minerals Act. Anybody wishing to mine atomic minerals has to get permission under this Act and follow the rules and precautions laid down by the AEC. There is therefore no need for an extra layer of approvals and FDI approval can be automatic 100 per cent.

If these suggestions are accepted all mining will be on the 100 per cent automatic route.

5.3.7.3 Infrastructure

Foreign equity in airports is already allowed up to 100 per cent but anything between 75 per cent and 100 per cent has to go through the FIPB route. Even 100 per cent foreign equity should be made automatic as no specific purpose is served by FIPB scrutiny in this heavily regulated sector.

Oil and gas pipelines have a "natural monopoly" element but this is quite weak because oil and gas can and are routinely transported by rail and road in direct competition with pipelines. This contrasts with other capital-intensive sectors such as power transmission where there is currently no other competitive alternative. As in the case of transmission a well-designed, optimally used gas/oil pipeline system can reduce capital costs and improve economic efficiency/competitiveness. With 100 per cent foreign equity allowed in power transmission (and other pipelines), the arguments against allowing the same in oil and gas pipelines are weak. These pipelines are regulated by the government and will come under the purview of an independent regulator in due course. We therefore recommend 100 per cent foreign equity under the automatic route.

The telecom sector foreign equity cap of 49 per cent may have reduced FDI inflows even though foreign investors can own another 49 per cent in a company that hold the remaining

51 per cent equity. Even in existing joint ventures between domestic and foreign companies, management can vest either with the domestic or foreign partner or both. Any change in management control is in general subject to the 'Takeover Rules and Regulations,' and these have been evolving over time to account for different possibilities. This process will continue. Security aspects of foreign investment in telecom are taken care of through a security clearance procedure and these can and should apply whatever the level of foreign equity. If necessary they can be modified and/or strengthened. The time has therefore come, in our view to revise the foreign equity cap on basic and mobile services upwards to 74 per cent. Along with this equity caps on radio paging, end-to-end bandwidth and internet gateways can be raised from 74 per cent to 100 per cent. These three along with voice mail, e-mail and ISP can be put on automatic route (subject to security clearance).

The entry of private airlines into the domestic aviation sector initially helped improve the quality of even Indian Airlines. The quality and competitiveness of domestic civil aviation can be improved on a sustainable basis by the entry of foreign airlines. The current ban on foreign airlines participation in joint ventures is not possible to justify on rational economic grounds. The foreign equity cap on civil aviation should be raised to 49 per cent (from 40 per cent) and foreign airlines allowed to invest within this cap. The 49 per cent limit represents below majority holding unlike 40 per cent, which has no link to any other limit or rule.

The experience of opening of terrestrial TV has demonstrated that private domestic and foreign entry is beneficial for citizens in terms of both information access and consumer choice. Direct to Home (DTH) broadcasting competes with terrestrial TV transmissions and is a competitive service with high capital costs and risks. Given the current 20 per cent foreign equity limit (KU band) foreign companies have little or no interest in entering this sector. This limit should be raised to 49 per cent (KU band etc.) so that foreign companies with the capital, technical competence and risk appetite can enter the country.

5.3.7.4 Services

There is scope for greater FDI inflow in the insurance sector if the cap of 26 per cent foreign equity is raised. The experience of opening up of this sector to FDI has set at rest the fears that were expressed earlier regarding the effect of such opening. The public insurance monopolies have responded to private entry by trying to increase their efficiency and effectiveness. This process would be enhanced and sustained by more effective competition. The regulatory system is in place and the Insurance Regulatory Authority (IRDA) is functioning effectively. The Committee feels that foreign equity cap can now be raised to 49 per cent.

With a large and mature banking system about 80 per cent of whose assets are in the public sector, the entire private sector is a relatively small player. Despite this the private sector has introduced new products and processes into banking and forced the public sector banks to compete in these areas. This process would be accelerated and enhanced if the FDI limits for private banks are raised from 49 per cent to 100 per cent, as few new foreign players have entered so far. With RBI recognized as one of the most competent regulators in the country, both domestic and foreign entrants can be effectively regulated. Given effective regulation, the entry of large foreign banks will enhance competition in the private banking and eliminate any temporary monopolies that may have arisen with innovation.

The minimum investment norms for FDI investment in Non-Bank Financial Companies no longer serve a useful purpose (as all NBFCs have to satisfy regulatory norms) and should be deleted. Similarly the equity limits on investing companies (for infrastructure and social sectors) should be raised to 100 per cent (from 49 per cent) and put on the automatic route.

100 per cent foreign equity is already allowed in courier services and this can be transferred to the automatic route. Consideration should also be given to bringing these services under the TRAI or the new regulator to be set up under the convergence bill.

There is currently a 74 per cent cap on foreign equity even though this is on the automatic route. Advertising is a creative process critically dependent on the creative human resources working in the company. Advertising requires a knowledge and understanding of culture that nationals always have a natural advantage. Similarly the relative salary levels that need to be paid to Indian nationals are significantly lower than nationals from richer countries. Because of both cultural understanding and salary differentials the creative and other professional workers critical to advertising are bound to be largely Indian. There is no need to insist on 26 per cent Indian equity. We therefore recommend that 100 per cent FDI be permitted in the advertising sector.

The real estate and housing sector has a globally demonstrated potential for attracting FDI. Though 100 per cent foreign equity is automatically allowed in the development of urban infrastructure and townships, only NRI/OCBs have the same facility as far as real estate and housing is concerned. Opening up of the real estate and housing sector to FDI investors can attract significant amount of FDI. Automatic 100 per cent equity could be allowed in industrial, commercial and residential complexes (covering one acre or more), while below this size and in the case of individual properties FDI could come through the FIPB route.

100 per cent FDI has recently been approved in tea plantations so that the considerable capital requirements of this sector can be met. In the absence of risk capital, the quality of output from these plantations has been deteriorating. Liberalization of FDI is similarly warranted in other plantations so that greater amount of risk capital is available for raising the productivity and output quality. We recommend a lower equity limit of 49 per cent for two reasons. There was 100 per cent foreign equity in many tea plantations at and after Independence right till the forced disinvestment in the seventies. Other (non-tea) plantations are generally smaller with

a much larger proportion owned by small farmers. A gradual approach that allows these owners to bring in foreign equity while retaining majority ownership is therefore preferable.

There is currently a somewhat complicated regime for FDI in non-retail trading. Automatic 100 per cent FDI is allowed in bulk handling, storage and transport of food and 51 per cent in export trading. 100 per cent equity is also allowed through the FIPB route in SSI products, hi-tech products, e-commerce (with 26 per cent disinvestments in 5 years), cash and carry wholesaling and warehousing. At least as far as these permitted areas of trading are concerned the regime should be simplified by allowing 100 per cent foreign equity through the automatic route with clearly spelt out conditions (if any). The retail sector in India is dispersed, widespread, labour intensive and disorganised. In the light of this it is not thought desirable at present to lift the ban on FDI in retail trade.

The Committee also recommends that the exit barriers identified in Table 5.3.7b be removed.

TABLE – 5.3.7B

Exit Barriers to be Considered for Deletion

1. Sale of shares by foreigner to another foreigner (FIPB-sectoral caps)	Remove
2. Sale from non-resident to resident (RBI permission)	Remove
3. Share SWAP permission-separate permission for share sale	Remove
4. Premium on publicly listed share price cannot exceed 25%	Remove
5. Share sale price (unlisted companies): Min (Book value, PE multiple method)'	Remove
6. Borrowing not allowed to purchase shares	No change

5.4 Marketing India

The problem at the screening stage needs to be seriously addressed *through improving the image of India, marketing India and conveying a positive approach towards FDI to foreign investors.* According to BCG, unhappy encounters would have to be replaced by success stories.

5.4.1 Attitude to FDI

An attitudinal and mind set change towards FDI is necessary. This may be conceptually simple but practically difficult to change; changing foreign perception of India and making India an attractive destination for FDI is a daunting challenge. The only method that is known to have worked in other countries is a clear and unambiguous message from the top leadership of the government conveying its importance to all organs of government. An alternative could be a well-designed publicity campaign bringing out the advantages that various countries have reaped from FDI.

5.4.2 India's Image

5.4.2.1 Advantages/Positives

Surveys have identified several advantages offered by India to FDI investment. These "Business Sweet Spots," need to be capitalised on (BCG). Among the advantages clearly perceived by existing and potential FDI investors are, higher skills, competitive wages and market size (ATK 2001). With respect to market size, it is however, necessary to be realistic given the low average per capita income. In the case of luxury products the market potential lies in the future and we should not oversell this advantage.

Studies have also shown that foreign invested companies in India have higher returns than in any other region. This is perhaps one of the reasons that a very high proportion of existing FDI want to carry out further investment in India (FICCI). Knowledge and experience of operating in India reduces the perceived risk making the return-risk trade off highly attractive. The success stories of Multi National Companies operating in India need to be documented and made known to potential investors. Officials of these Multi National Companies should also be involved in helping market India to other potential investors.

Other advantages include government incentives and opportunities in infrastructure development. This information needs to be made widely known to potential infrastructure investors. India's tax regime for exporters and export production has been one of the most transparently favourable for at least a decade. Yet few potential investors are aware of the tax regime, because we have not publicised it appropriately, for instance by comparing it with the taxes in favoured FDI destinations.

5.4.2.2 Inconveniences/Negatives

There are also many actual and perceived disadvantages facing FDI in India that must be addressed on in any marketing effort. In one survey 54 per cent of the respondents said that India's structural inconveniences do not exceed that of other emerging markets (ATK 2001). Yet these disadvantages are cited in the media much more often with respect to India than with respect to other countries.[28]

FDI investors perceive a high degree of uncertainty in India. This includes political and administrative uncertainty, legal delays and bureaucratic delays. This translates into a higher risk perception than is perhaps warranted. To the extent that actual risk differs from the perceived risk, the best antidote is better and more authentic information. Thus for instance research

28. If the Pfefferman/IFC study is valid, investors are finally beginning to see through the veil created by the media.

institutions should publish objective measures of risk such as the variance of returns. Comparative studies on risk-return trade-off should also be helpful. Available studies and success stories should be publicised.

5.4.3 *Revamping Publicity*

The government must take steps to provide more and better information about policy, regulations, procedures etc., as relevant to each sector. This could be done through a web site designed with the specific objective of facilitating foreign and domestic investment but designed keeping in mind the special difficulties perceived by potential foreign direct investors relatively unfamiliar with India.

A strong publicity mechanism needs to be put in place, which can project success stories in various sectors. The administrative ministries have an important role to play in this regard. While it is most important to remove real constraints to investment, it is equally important to remove coloured perceptions that prospective investors may have about India as an investment destination. For example, on the issue of policy uncertainty, which is often cited as a negative feature of India, it has to be emphasised that there has been only one incident of major policy reversal since 1991. The recent spurt in FDI inflows also requires to be projected prominently as an indicator of growing investor confidence. Similarly, some of the sector initiatives taken by the Government such as the National Mineral policy, the Biotech Park scheme, power sector reforms, disinvestments, need to be publicised more effectively. India has one of the most liberal and transparent FDI regimes as noted by several informed observers.[29] This fact needs to be publicised.

5.4.4 *Marketing Strategy*

The Foreign Investment Promotion Council (FIPC) should be transformed into the primary arm of the government for promoting FDI in India, with the Department of Industrial Policy and Promotion (DIPP) continuing to act as its secretariat.[30] The Chairman of the FIPC could be a person of national and international credibility. The membership of FIPC should include finance person, an economist, a legal expert, and the secretary (IPP) as an ex-officio member. There should also be provision for two part-time members from the industry. The organisation should target specific corporations and interact with the CEO and boards of these companies for enticing them to take investment decisions in favour of India. Besides the authority should also constitute half a dozen special groups headed by Ministers or Minister level functionaries

29. This was acknowledged by Mr. Pascal Lamy, EU Trade Commissioner, during his recent visit to India.
30. An alternative would be to transform this into a registered society so that there can be more equal public-private partnership in marketing and facilitation of FDI.

who could be earmarked a set of companies with whom they have to establish contact.

The existing approach to providing information and generic promotion of FDI to India needs to be complemented by a sector and firm specific marketing strategy. We should make a short list of potential investors and develop a customised sales pitch for each of them. Based on this a business focused discussion should be held with the real decision makers. For such an approach to be effective we must understand the fundamental and specific needs of each of the targeted investors. Only then can we help them work out concrete investment proposals. At the problem solving stage the right ministries, concerned State governments and other relevant institutions must be available around the table to find solutions and make quick decisions.

A start can be made by collecting and analysing information on the activities and foreign investments of the 500 largest trans-national companies. The analysis would identify the sectors of interest to each of these 500 companies. This could be followed by the setting up of sector specific high-level special groups and the apportioning of the 500 companies among them according to their likely sector of interest in India. This would include sectors like electronics and computers, machinery and equipment (including electrical), chemicals and cosmetics, motor vehicles and parts, food and beverages and services (utilities, telecom, media, publishing, retailing, trading) and other manufacturing (paper, packaging, rubber/tyres, steel, construction materials). Marketing expertise should be drawn upon by the special groups in devising a strategy for contacting and persuading each of these companies to make large investments in India.

5.5 Policy for Special Economic Zones

China's success in attracting export related FDI and its success in labour intensive exports contrasts sharply with that of India. Many of the policy reforms that are politically difficult in India were equally difficult in China. China however was able to introduce these reforms on an experimental basis in their Special Export Zones and then use the demonstrated success of these reforms to make them deeper and wider.[31] This is an example worth emulating.[32]

5.5.1 State SEZ Law(s)

We would recommend that States consider enactment of a Special Economic Zone (SEZ) law that would apply to all SEZs in the State. The Maharashtra SEZ law can be used as a basis or a possible model for this purpose. The law should cover State level industrial, labour, environmental, infrastructure and administrative issues, with a view to simplifying and promoting investment and production in the SEZs.

31. One of the members has informed that a separate exercise is underway in M/o C&I to develop proposals for "competitive zones," which would cover much of this recommendation.

32. Current state of SEZs is given in appendix section 7.4.

5.5.2 SEZ Infrastructure Policy

Though it will take a decade or more to improve infrastructure services across the country, infrastructure availability and quality can be brought to global standards in the Special Economic Zones (SEZs) within a couple of years. The effect of a weak highway and railway system can be minimised by locating SEZs in the coastal regions as was done by China and many other countries in South East Asia. Among the measures needed for accelerated development of infrastructure in and exports from SEZs are;

a. Power generation and distribution for the SEZ needs to be isolated from the problem ridden SEBs to the extent possible. As size limitations make electricity generation for the SEZ alone, non-optimal, the private electricity generator for the SEZ should be allowed to sell excess power to parties outside the SEZ subject to transparent wheeling charges and cross tax-subsidy arrangement.

b. There should be free entry and exit of telecom service providers into the SEZ without any service or USO charges, subject only to the condition that the spectrum would be auctioned if and only if it ceases to be a "free good" within the SEZ. In the case of spectrum used for GSM this will happen when the number of mobile operators reaches four. Inter-connectivity with other countries (international long distance) should be free and unrestricted (subject only to the condition that this cannot be used as a conduit for provision of unregulated telecom services into the Domestic Tariff Area (DTA). Automatic 100 per cent FDI should be allowed.

c. Private parties would also be free to set up a private airport or port to service the SEZs (FDI is already automatic 100 per cent). If an unused harbour is not available nearby, the requisite number of berths in the closest port should be made available to private parties for the purpose of servicing the SEZ. These parties or another developer should be given the authority to set up toll highway connecting the port to the SEZ.

d. A law should be passed by the State governments under which 100 per cent privately owned townships could be set up and run by private developers as private municipalities. Private SEZs should be designated as private municipalities under this law and road, electricity transmission and other linkages provided by State/Central government.

5.5.3 SEZ Administrative Structure

A number of other legal and bureaucratic changes can also be introduced much more quickly in the SEZs than is possible in the country in general. The applicable laws, rules, regulations and procedures in the SEZs should be made as attractive as in China's coastal regions and other competing destinations. In fact we should experiment with an even bolder model of a market economy in which traditional controls and restrictions are replaced by a modern regulatory system based on trust that punishes violators quickly and effectively like the traffic light approach.[33] This requires,

a. Elimination of all price controls and distribution controls (e.g. on power, rent),

b. Removal of all investment restrictions (e.g. SSI reservation, foreign equity limits and bans, public sector reservation) for production and supply within the zone or for export. This would include removal of State and local restrictions (eg. urban land ceiling, retail trade, real estate).

c. Removal of all capital account restrictions/controls/prior permissions for businesses operating within the SEZ (reporting requirements and regulations relating to inflow of foreign exchange debt etc. into DTA would remain).

d. International standard financial regulations for financial institutions operating within the zone with Indian "controls"eliminated. Thus the FDI limits on banking, insurance, NBFCs would not apply, directed credit and SLR would be eliminated and CRR brought down to internationally comparable levels.

e. Customs, excise and service tax laws to be modified so that all transactions within the SEZ are exempt and transaction of DTA with the SEZ can be treated as if with a foreign country. Normal excise (& customs) rules would no longer apply for transactions within the SEZs. Customs and Additional duty (equal to CENVAT/Excise) and SAD would apply to all sales to DTA.[34] State sales tax law should also be modified, so that within the SEZ only sales to resident consumers, not producers/traders are taxed. No excise/CST/ST/Octroi would be charged for sales from DTA to SEZs.

f. SEZs should be exempt from MAT and dividend tax. All export related profits should be exempt from corporate income tax for a specified period.

g. A new labour law incorporating a work ethic and including abolition of Contract Labour restrictions be enacted/prescribed. The law may also provide for freedom for multiple and night shift for workers of both sexes. The Development Commissioner may be designated as Labour Commissioner.

h. An integrated unified industrial regulator, with authority under industrial regulations, pollution, labour safety and other laws delegated to him. The number of specialised inspectors should be reduced to a minimum.

---

33. For some regulations self certification may be adequate while for others outside (private) certification (e.g. by an accredited professional or certification agency) may be required.

34. SAD should not however apply if state sales and other taxes apply.

i. The Development Commissioner may be designated as the Commissioner under all the relevant laws (industrial, environmental etc.) within the SEZ.

j. A special court for SEZ(s) that deals with cases arising in the SEZ equipped with all modern facilities, that can deal with cases in a time bound manner.

5.5.4 Marketing of SEZs

A special marketing effort is needed for export oriented FDI. For instance, Taiwanese and other exporters in East and South East Asia can be targeted for this purpose. Our missions in OECD and other FDI source countries should be fully briefed on the comparative advantages of SEZs in India and distribute the required literature.

5.6 Sector Policy Reforms

Domestic policies and regulations determine the environment for private investment. This environment affects both domestic investors and FDI. Simplification and modernisation of laws, rules and regulations, eliminations of controls and bans, introduction of a modern professional regulatory systems and other policy reforms will result in greater gross domestic investment. These measures will also increase the flow of FDI. A few of the policy issues that can have a relatively larger effect on FDI vis-a-vis indigenous investment are discussed below.

5.6.1 Disinvestment

Across the world, disinvestment has acted as a magnet for FDI. Though foreign companies are allowed to bid for government strategic share sale, there is some apprehension about doing so. If a clear signal is given that foreign companies are not only allowed but also encouraged to bid in disinvestment auctions, this could attract a significant amount of FDI. This in turn means that additional outside capital and investment will flow into industry from outside the system rather than existing private investment moving from one industry or sector to another. FDI flow into privatisation is more likely to be complimentary, strategic purchase by domestic investors may have some element of substitution. As the strategic sale route has now crystallised into a transparent, time-bound, non-discretionary process, FDI investors should have confidence in the mechanism. A well-programmed "Road Show" for large value high profile disinvestments to target FDI should be encouraged.

5.6.2 Power

Private investment in the power sector, both domestic and FDI, depends on power sector reform. Policy and regulatory reform, relating to user charges, reduction of theft and private entry into distribution are a pre-requisite for increased private investment. Without such reforms

FDI and domestic investment in the power sector will remain a trickle. The Electricity Bill, currently before Parliament, lays down a framework for private entry into and competition in this sector. Remaining weakness in the Bill can be taken up once there is some experience of its operation.

Privatisation of the existing generating capacity along with open access to the transmission-distribution system subject to explicit cross-tax subsidy and the setting up of a competitive market could also attract substantial FDI and private domestic investment. Complete decontrol of new investment in power generation and distribution in rural areas can also be experimented with to free entrepreneurs from the vice like grip of legacy systems. Besides stand-alone systems this may also require open access to the existing rural electricity distribution system.

5.6.3 Urban Infrastructure and Real Estate

It is estimated that removing land market barriers can contribute an additional 1 per cent to India's GDP growth rate (McKinsey 2001). There is an urgent need to ensure compulsory registration of land deeds and also to computerize such records so as to create a database of such records. The Andhra Pradesh experience is a good example to begin with where registration of sale of land/property is achieved within a month. The monopoly of urban development agencies over land should be replaced by greater competition within the master plan of the city. The Centre has repealed the Urban Land Ceiling Act, but only a half a dozen States have notified its repeal. Other States should also do so.

The Rent Control Act is probably the single most important cause for the existence of metropolitan slums, as building rental housing for low and middle-income groups amounts to gifting one's assets. States should repeal the Rent Control Act for all new tenancies and phase it out for existing tenancies. Our urban and municipal laws and regulations date back to half a century if not more. There is a need to thoroughly review and modernize them in the light of the latest developments in urban infrastructure, transport, pollution control etc. A system of deemed approvals for all planning permissions by registered architects operating on a self-regulatory basis, much like chartered accountants, would enormously speed up the entire process and ensure far larger quantum of housing stock are supplied every year, at more reasonable prices than is the case so far.

Urban taxes such as property tax, stamp duty on sale of land and buildings and entertainment tax need to be rationalised. Creation of Real Estate Mutual Funds/Real Estate Investment Trusts should be permitted. Development of the secondary mortgage market and securitisation of loan assets will increase the liquidity position of the housing finance companies and make available funds at low cost. Foreclosure laws to be passed- this will enable financiers to repossess properties without having to seek recourse from courts.

An urban reforms facility has been set up by the Central government to provide an incentive to States to carry out these reforms, which fall largely under their purview.

5.6.4 De-control and De-licensing

De-control of the petroleum (oil, gas etc.), coal and small industry sectors needs to be completed to stimulate efficiency and productivity improvement and investment. The Petroleum Regulation Law should move decisively from the control-oriented approach of the seventies and eighties to the adoption of the competitive approach that characterises industrial development in the nineties. A regulatory system is needed only for the 'natural monopoly' segments such as oil and gas pipelines. Such a modern system can also be given authority to cover specified situations (such as war and natural disaster) and specified regions (such as North-East and Jammu and Kashmir) requiring special attention because of their remoteness.

A number of items with export potential have recently been removed from the list of SSI reserved items and the investment limit raised for items where the technology requires greater investment to attain Minimum Efficient Scale (MES). Over 700 items however remain on the list. SSI reservation should be phased out as quickly as possible. Limits on equity holding by companies in SSI units should be removed so that those units who require equity for growth are not constrained by the weak access of small units to the capital market. Factor markets (management, labour) liberalisation also needs to proceed forward.

5.6.5 Tax Rules and Rates

Many countries, such as Malaysia, Thailand and China have had at various times, tax rates that favour foreign direct investment over domestic direct investment. Our tax laws treat all companies incorporated in India equally, irrespective of the proportion of foreign equity holding (national treatment). Tax rates have however often been higher in the case of Indian branches of foreign incorporated companies (eg. foreign airlines and banks operating in India through such branches). They have recently been reduced from 48 per cent to 42 per cent (40 per cent with 5 per cent surcharge). These rates should be reduced to the effective rate of 36.5 per cent applicable to companies (registered in India). There is also a clear case for making tax laws and rules as simple and internationally comparable for FDI. In contrast the benefit-cost ratio from providing favourable tax treatment to foreign direct investors vis-à-vis domestic investors is less clear. Lower rates for FDI can however be considered in selected high technology sectors (that will benefit the country), as they can act as a signalling device to attract attention to opportunities that may have been missed otherwise.

Both domestic and foreign investment would also be encouraged by a reduction in the corporate tax rate (35 per cent) to the highest marginal rate on personal income (30 per cent).

6

Concluding Summary

The major recommendations of the Steering Committee can be summarised as follows:

- Consider the enactment of a Foreign Investment Promotion Law that incorporates and integrates aspects relevant to promotion of FDI [section 5.1.1]
- Urge States to enact a special investment law relating to Infrastructure to expedite all investment in infrastructure sectors and remove hurdles to production in this critical sector [section 5.1.2]
- Empower the Foreign Investment Promotion Board to give initial Central level registrations and approvals where possible, with a view to speeding up the process of project implementation [section 5.2].
- Change government's Rules of Business to empower FIIA to expedite the processing of administrative and policy approvals [section 5.2.1].
- The aggregate FDI target for the 10th Plan should be disaggregated in terms of sectors and relevant administrative ministries/department, to increase accountability. This could help ensure that the policy pre-requisites for increasing domestic private investment and FDI are expedited by the concerned departments [section 5.2.2].
- Sectoral FDI caps should be reduced to the minimum and entry barriers eliminated. With the exception of 'Defence industry' FDI caps can be removed in all manufacturing and mining. Caps can also be eliminated in Advertising, Private Banks and Real Estate and raised in Telecom, Civil Aviation, DTH/KU broadcasting, Insurance and Plantations (other than tea)[section 5.3].
- The existing strategy for attracting FDI should be overhauled. The relative emphasis must shift from a broad (scatter shot) approach to one of targeting specific companies

in specific sectors. The Foreign Investment Promotion Council should be reformed to implement this strategy. It should be chaired by a person with global credibility and involve Minister level functionaries who can interact with the heads of the Fortune 500 companies. [section 5.4.4]

- The informational aspects of the strategy should be refined in the light of the perceived advantages and disadvantages of India as an investment destination and should use information technology and modern marketing techniques [section 5.4.1, 5.4.2]
- The Special Economic Zones should be developed as the most competitive destination for export related FDI in the world, by simplifying applicable laws, rules, and administrative procedures and reducing red tape to the levels found in China. The focus should be on accelerated/immediate implementation of reforms that may take a much longer time [e.g. decade(s)] in the country as whole and *not* on tax sops [section 5.5].
- Domestic Policy Reforms in the Power Sector, Urban Infrastructure and Real Estate and de-control/de-licensing should be expedited to promote private domestic and foreign investment [section 5.6].

7

References

Government of India (2001), Office of Economic Adviser, Ministry of Commerce & Industry, *Handbook of Industrial Policy and Statistics*, 2000, New Delhi.

—— (2002) Development of Industrial Policy and Promotion, Ministry of Commerce and Industry, *Investment in India, 2002*, New Delhi.

—— (2001), Department of Industrial Policy & Promotion, Ministry of Commerce and Industry, *Manual on Industrial Policy & Procedures in India*, 2002, New Delhi.

—— (2002) Department of Industrial Policy & Promotion, Ministry of Commerce and Industry, *Indian Special Economic Zones, Investors' Guide, 2002*, New Delhi.

—— (2002), Department of Economic Affairs, Ministry of Finance, *Economic Survey 2001-02*, New Delhi.

—— (2001), Planning Commission, *Approach Paper to the Tenth Five Year Plan (2002-07)*, New Delhi.

UNCTAD, United Nations, *World Investment Report 1997: Transnational Corporations, Market Structure and Competition Policy*, New York, 1997.

—— (1998) *World Investment Report, 1998: Trends and Determinants*, New York, 1998.

—— (1999), *World Investment Report, 1999: Foreign Direct Investment and the Challenge of Development*, United Nations, New York, 1999.

—— (2000), *World Investment Report, 2000*, New York, 2000.

—— (2001), *World Investment Report, 2001*, New York, 2001.

World Bank, *World Development Report* (several issues),

Reserve Bank of India (2002), *Report on Currency & Finance, 2000-01*, Bombay

—— (2001), *Handbook of Statistics on Indian Economy*, Bombay, 2001.

India Investment Centre (IIC), Foreign Investment Policy, May 1997, New Delhi.

National Council of Applied Economic Research (NCAER), *Foreign Direct Investment in India*, March 1998, New Delhi.

Confederation of Indian Industry (CII), 2002, *From Crumbs to Riches: Reorienting Foreign Direct Investment in India, 2002*, New Delhi.

—— Foreign Direct Investment in India : How can $ 10 billion of Annual Inflows be Realized, (*Sachs, Jeffrey D, Nirupam, Bajpai, Mark F. Blaxill, Arun Maira)*, New Delhi, January 2000.

—— *The Malaysian Industrial Development Authority: A Suggested Model, 2002*, New Delhi.

Federation of Indian Chambers of Commerce & Industry (FICCI), 2001, *The Experience of Foreign Direct Investors in India*, April, 2001, New Delhi.

A.T. Kearney, Inc. (2001), Global Business Policy Council, *FDI Confidence Audit: India*, Alxandric, Virginia, USA, 2001.

McKinsey & Company (2001), Identifying the Barriers to Rapid Employment and Output Growth in India, McKinsey Global Institute, New York., June 2001.

—— Achieving Quantum Leap in India's FDI, McKinsey Global Institute, New York, June 2001

Centre for Monitoring Indian Economy (CMIE), 2002, *Problems & Progress in Implementation of Major Investment Projects in India*, (based on a survey undertaken on behalf of Department of Industrial Policy and Promotion, Oct.-2001) January, 2002, Bombay.

Administrative Staff College of India, 1999, *Simplification of Procedures Governing Industries* (A study undertaken on behalf of the Department of Industrial Policy & Promotion, Ministry of Commerce and Industry, (Government of India)), Hyderabad, December, 1999.

Government of Andhra Pradesh, *Andhra Pradesh Infrastructure Development Enabling Act, 2001*, Andhra Pradesh Gazette, Sept. 5, 2001, Hyderabad.

Indian Institute of Foreign Trade (IIFT), 1990, Foreign Investment Law and Policy in Select Developing Countries, June, 1990, New Delhi.

Agarwala, Ramgopala, The Rise of China: Threat or Opportunity, Research and Information System for the Non-aligned and other Developing Countries, 2002, New Delhi.

Bhoi, B.K., *Merger & Acquisition: An Indian Experience,* Occasional Papers Reserve Bank of India, Vol.21, No.1, Summer 2000, Bombay.

Gokarn, Subir, *The Essence of Zones,* Business Standard, Vol.XXV No.5, April 3, 2000, New Delhi.

Kumar, Nagesh and Jaya Pradhan, Foreign Direct Investment, *Externalities and Economic Growth in Developing Countries,* RIS Discussion Papers, Research and Information System for the Non-Aligned and other Developing Countries, April, 2002.

Kumar, Nagesh, *WTO's Emerging Investment Regime :Way Forward for Doha Ministerial Meeting*, Economic & Political Weekly, Vol.XXXVI, No.33, August 18, 2001, Bombay.

—— Merger & Acquisition by MNEs : *Pattern & Implications*, Economic and Political Weekly, Vol.XXXV, No.32, August 5, 2000, Bombay.

Mandal R, *Privatization in the Third World*, Vikas Publishing House, 1994, New Delhi.

Thomas, T., *Stepping up FDI*, Business Standard, Vol.VII, No.115, August 30, 2000, New Delhi.

—— *The Industrial Promotion Board*, Business Standard, December 3, 2001, New Delhi.

Patnaik, Prabhat, *Investment and Growth in a Liberalized Economy*, Lecture at LBSNAA (mimio), Mussorrie, June, 1994.

Virmani A, India's 1990-91 *Crisis: Reforms, Myths and Paradoxes*, Working Paper Series, Paper No.4/2001-PC, Planning Commission, December 2001, New Delhi.

8

Appendices

8.1 Economic Advantages of FDI

Foreign direct investment brings in investible resources to host countries, introduces modern technologies and provides access to export markets. The trans-national companies (TNCs/MNEs) are the driving force behind foreign direct investment. They have large internal (inter-firm) markets, access to which is available only to affiliates. They also control large markets in unrelated parties *having established brand names and distribution channels spread over several national locations.* They can, thus, influence granting of trade privileges in their home (or in third) markets. In other words, they enjoy considerable advantages in creating an initial export base for new entrants.

While there are TNCs/MNEs with sales turnover larger than the national incomes of many developing countries, there are also many new entrants, which are *small and medium sized enterprises (SMEs).* Many of these firms find it necessary to invest overseas to overcome lack of opportunities for growth at home, access skilled labour abroad and reduce cost. An increasing number of such firms are from developing countries. Some of these firms belong to 'economies in transition' that previously had isolated themselves from international investment. As a result, the number of MNEs has increased substantially and is estimated to have gone up to more than 50,000 by the end of the 1990's. Between the end of 1960's and the end of 1990's, the number of MNEs in fifteen of the most important developed countries itself had gone up from 7000 to 40,000. FDI inflows mirror this expansion that has gone up from an investment level of $ 56 billion at the beginning of the 1980's to $ 693 billion in 1998. *It reached an investment level of $ 188 billion in developing countries alone.*

The changing context and the quest for location for manufacture and trade have brought about a change in corporate strategies. According to the UNCTAD, United Nations (1999), following developments are particularly noteworthy:

- A shift from stand-alone, relatively independent, foreign affiliates to *integrated international production systems* relying on specialized affiliates to service the entire TNC/MNE system. Within the framework of this international intra-firm division of labour, any part of the value-added chain of an enterprise can be located abroad while remaining fully integrated into a corporate network. Corporate strategies of this kind seek to exploit regional or global economies of scale and a higher degree of functional specialization.
- This shift broadens the range of resources sought by MNEs in host countries, making firms more selective in their choices. However, it can also encourage FDI in countries that cannot provide a wide range of resources but have some specific assets that are sought by MNEs (e.g. *accounting or software skills*).
- A shift towards greater use of *non-equity and cooperative relationships* with other enterprises, such as *alliances, partnerships, management contracts or sub-contracting arrangements.* These arrangements serve a variety of corporate objectives. They can provide better access to technologies or other assets allowing firms to share the cost and risk of innovatory activities. They can reduce the production cost of labour-intensive products.
- Emerging of a network type of organization. This expands the scope of interactions between TNCs and enterprises from host countries, and also the forms of these interactions.

These changing corporate strategies bring a different pattern of international economic integration. Originally, this involved the integration of markets through arm's length trade — "shadow" integration. *Integrated international production moves this integration to the level of production in all its aspects — "deep" integration.* In the process, a significant part of international transactions becomes internalized, i.e. takes the form of transactions between various parts of transnational corporate systems located in different countries. The ability of firms to allocate their economic assets internationally, and the international production system created in the process, have become themselves a part of the new context.

Crowding-in and crowding-out impacts of FDI

Crowding-in is said to take place when foreign direct investment stimulates new investment in downstream or upstream production by other foreign or domestic producers. While investments in the export sector has the potential for encouraging downstream production, investments in infrastructure encourage upstream production. The TNCs/MNEs may provide preferential opportunity for exports through access to large internal (inter-firm) markets, which is available only to affiliates set up in host countries. The capital-flow induced growth and the accompanying higher efficiency of the economy may, in turn, induce higher investments.

However, if FDI comes in sectors in which the domestic firms are themselves contemplating investment, the very act of foreign investment may take away the investment opportunities that were open to domestic enterprises. Moreover, if the TNCs/MNEs raised funds for their expansion programmes from the host country, this might out-compete the domestic firms in the financial markets and thus compete them out. The decision of TNCs/MNEs for acquisition (M&A) of domestic firms might similarly lead to large inflow of foreign exchange, appreciating in the process the exchange rate. This might in turn make the host country's export less competitive and thus discourage domestic investment for export markets. All these imperatives may have crowding-out impact on domestic firms.

In regard to the net impact of the crowding-in and crowding-out of FDI, the UNCTAD, United Nations (1999) observed, 'In an early example, relating to Canada, of the few studies addressing the question, some regression coefficient, taken at face value implied that $1 of direct investment led to $3 of capital formation' (Lubitz, 1966). A later study of FDI in Canada (Van Loo, 1977), with somewhat different methods, a slightly longer time span and annual rather than quarterly data, found a positive direct effect on capital formation greater than the amount of the FDI. That is, in addition, to FDI effect on investment, there was some complimentary effect on fixed investment by domestic firms. However, when indirect effects through other variables, such as exports (negative), imports (positive) and consumption (negative), operating through the accelerator was added, the addition to total capital formation was much smaller, a little over half the inflow'.

It has been, further observed, 'A recent study of the impact of FDI on economic growth, utilizing data on FDI inflows from developed countries to 69 developing countries on a yearly basis from 1970 to 1989, has found, among others, that FDI has stimulated domestic investment: "a one dollar increase in the net flow of FDI is associated with an increase in total investment in the host economy of more than one dollar. The value of the point estimates place the total increase in investment between 1.5 and 2.3 times the increase in the flow of FDI" (Borensztain, et al, 1995).

In view of the double edged nature of FDI, namely, the crowding-out and crowding-in effects on domestic industries, the host economies especially the developing countries have been imposing some kind of *performance requirements* in regard to: (a) local content (b) export commitment (c) technology transfer (d) dividend balancing and (e) foreign exchange neutrality. These regulations have been there to enhance the quality of FDI against the simple increase in the quantity of FDI inflow. Imposition of *performance criteria*, however, comes in the way of *the relative openness of the trade regime* and may make FDI less attractive for MNEs while deciding the location for their operations. In other words, a trade-off is involved between PERFORMANCE and OPENNESS.

Crowding-in took place in the case of Argentina's communications privatisation, where the development of domestic sub contractors was part and parcel of the privatisation agreement with foreign investors and appears to be working well. Countries in East Asia, namely, Indonesia, Malaysia and Thailand encouraged FDI in microelectronics related items like toys and other consumer goods for export markets. Many of these foreign affiliates were essentially assemblers with few linkages to the rest of the economy. *Overtime, however, domestic suppliers of services and inputs have emerged.*

The UNCTAD, United Nations (1999), nevertheless, further remarked *there are also examples of economies that have chosen to stimulate domestic investment in new activities rather than to rely on FDI.* This was the rationale for limiting FDI in certain high-technology industries in the Republic of Korea and Taiwan Province of China. In these cases, the vision by policy makers that domestic firms could in fact emerge *paid off.* In many cases, however, the emergence of successful domestic producers in a new, technologically advanced industry is unlikely or might take a long time with uncertain results. An example of *a costly intervention* in favour of domestic firms in high-technology industries is the Brazilian Informatics policy of the early 1980's, which involved restrictions on FDI in information technology activities.

8.2 Need For FDI in 10th Plan

The Approach Paper to the Tenth Five Year Plan (2002-07) observes, 'Recognizing the importance of making a quantum jump compared with the past performance, the Prime Minister directed the Planning Commission to examine the feasibility of doubling per capita income in the next ten years. With the population expected to grow at about 1.6 per cent per annum, this target requires the growth of GDP to be around 8.7 per cent over the Tenth and Eleventh Plan periods.... *The Approach Paper proposes an indicative target of 8.0 per cent of growth for the year 2002-07.* This is lower than the growth rate of 8.7 per cent needed to double per capita income over the next ten years, but it can be viewed as an intermediate target *for the first half of the period'.*

With the average ICOR around 4.0 as witnessed during the Eighth and Ninth Plan periods, *the saving- investment requirement* for an 8 per cent annual growth *works out to 32 per cent of GDP,* since, Gr = 100 × s/k, s = Gr × k × 100 = .08 × 4 × 100= 32 per cent.

Where, Gr = Growth rate, s = average propensity to save/rate of investment, k = incremental capita output ratio (ICOR).

The rate of domestic savings has been in the range of 22-24 per cent of GDP during the last four years. These rates are lower than the earlier years, presumably due to decline in government savings on account of payment of arrears etc. arising from Fifth Pay Commission Recommendations. The base line savings rate has, therefore, been assumed to be 26.3 per cent (Table 8.2). This still leaves a gap of another 6.3 per cent to reach the 32.6 per cent of savings rate. Assuming further improvement, the Approach Paper has projected a domestic savings rate of 29.8 per cent of GDP, for the Tenth Plan period. *This still leaves a gap of 2.8 per cent for the required investment*. Quite obviously, this calls for sourcing foreign savings to bridge the gap.

TABLE – 8.2

Macroeconomic Parameters for the Tenth Plan

	Base Line	Target	Difference /Gap
I. Average GDP Growth Rate (% per annum)	6.5	8.0	+1.5
II. Gross Investment Rate (% of GDP at market price)	27.8	32.6	+4.8
III. Implicit ICOR	4.28	4.08	-0.20
IV. Gross Domestic Savings, of which	26.3	29.8	+3.5
(i) Government	-0.6	1.7	+2.3
(ii) Public Enterprises	3.0	2.9	-0.1
(iii) Private Corporate Sector	4.9	5.8	+0.9
(iv) Household Sector	19.0	19.4	+0.4
VI. Current Account Deficit (CAD)	1.5	2.8	+1.3

8.2.1 Foreign Savings and CAD

Foreign savings gap or current account deficit on the balance of payments (CAD), in turn, may be bridged through external assistance, external commercial borrowings, foreign investment flows (FDI and portfolio investment) and NRI deposits. Table 8.2.1a shows that FDI inflows, during the Ninth Plan, have been in the range of US$ 2-4 billion.

The Tenth Plan Approach Paper, on a cautious note, visualized FDI inflows in the range of 1-1.5% of GDP during the plan period. The *Sub-group on the External Sector for the Tenth Plan,* moreover, has the projections worked out for FDI inflows under two scenarios during the Plan as shown below (Table 8.2.1b).

Indeed, the achievement of 8 per cent of growth rate becomes contingent on higher FDI inflows *and the other two key variables, namely, increase in government savings and reduction in incremental value of capital-output ratio.*

TABLE – 8.2.1A

Sources of Foreign Savings

(in US $ million)

	97-98	98-99	99-00	2000-01	2001-02
(A) FDI (net)	3557	2462	2155	2339	3905
(B) Portfolio Investment (net)	1828	-61	3026	2760	2020
(C) ECB (net)	3999	4362	313	4011	-1144
(D) NRI Deposits (net)	1125	960	1540	2317	2754
(E) External Assistance (net)	907	820	901	427	1117

TABLE – 8.2.1B

FDI Projections for the Tenth Plan

(in US$ Million)

GDP Growth	2002-03	2003-04	2004-05	2005-06	2006-07	Average
(i) @ 6.5%	5400	6800	8200	9600	11000	8200
(ii) @ 8.0%	6500	8150	9800	11450	13100	9800

8.3 Policy Framework

8.3.1 Industrial Policy

Under the Industries (Development & Regulation Act), 1951, the Government of India has been notifying its Industrial Policy Statement from time to time. The policy statements, over the years, have been focused on the distinction between *the public sector enterprises* under the Central Government (Schedule I Industries), industries for which compulsory licensing is required (Schedule II Industries) and small scale/ancillary industries (Schedule III Industries).

The Industrial Policy Reform of 1991 marks a watershed as it introduced significant changes in the erstwhile industrial policy through pruning the list of industries reserved under Schedule I & II. Efforts towards further liberalization have since then continued.

Schedule III industries or small scale industries refer to industrial undertakings with investment in fixed assets (plants and machinery) not exceeding Rs.10 million. *As per the latest industrial policy, such units can manufacture any item and are also generally free from location restrictions imposed on Schedule I and II Industries.*

Over and above these there are *industries to the exclusion of Schedule I, II and III categories.* Industries, which may come up in EPZ/SEZ, moreover, qualify for a separate treatment.

In the case of all large and medium industries, exempt from the requirements of industrial licensing, information about the industrial undertaking ought to be filed before the commencement of production in the prescribed Industrial Entrepreneurs Memorandum (IEM) A-Form along with a demand draft of Rs.10,000/-. At the time of commencement of commercial production, moreover, the industrial undertaking needs to file information in the IEM, B-Form.

The Schedule II category of industries generally belongs to polluting and hazardous group of industries and therefore, calls for prior approval of the Central Government (or the State Government). The industry concerned thus has to submit the application in the prescribed form, i.e. Form FC-IL to the Entrepreneurial Assistance Unit (EAU) of the Secretariat of Industrial Assistance (SIA) of the Department of Industrial Policy and Promotion (DIPP), Ministry of Commerce & Industry. Approvals, if forthcoming, are normally conveyed within 4-6 weeks of submitting the application.

The Small Scale Industries, on the other hand, may get registered with the Directorate of Industries/District Industries Center of the State Government concerned. *Manufacture of items reserved for the small-scale sector can also be taken up by non-small scale units, if they apply for and obtain an industrial license* from the SIA/FIPB in the DIPP. In such cases, moreover, it is mandatory for the non-small scale unit *to undertake minimum export obligation of 50 percent.*

8.3.2 Project Clearance

After the approval has been obtained, the applicant may get his unit/company registered with the Registrar of Company. Subsequently, *the company needs to obtain various clearances such as, land clearance, building design clearance, pre construction clearance, labour clearance etc. from different authorities before beginning its operations.* These clearances, moreover, differ from sector to sector and may also differ from state to state.

8.3.2.1 Registration and Inspection

Each industrial unit is, moreover, supposed to maintain record in regard to production, sale and export, use of specified raw material including public utilities like water and electricity, labour related details, financial details and details in regard to industrial safety and environment.

The unit is also subject to periodic inspection by the factories inspector, labour inspector, food inspector, fire inspector, central excise inspector, air and water inspector, mines inspector, city inspector and the like, the list of which may go up to thirty or more.

8.3.3 FDI Policy

The above-mentioned industrial policy provisions hold good for both the domestic and foreign companies. Once the approval has been given to a foreign investor, namely, a multinational enterprise (MNE), an overseas corporate body (OCB) or a Non-Resident Indian (NRI), these companies are treated on par with any other Indian company (national treatment).

8.3.3.1 FEMA (2000)

The additional provisions, which apply only to entry of Foreign Direct Investment (FDI) emanate from the provisions of Foreign Exchange Management Act (FEMA), 2000. According to FEMA, 2000 no person resident outside India shall without the approval /knowledge of the Reserve Bank of India (RBI) may establish in India a branch or a liaison office or a project office or any other place of business.

FDI in a particular industry may, however, be made through *(a) the automatic route under powers delegated to the RBI or (b) the SIA route with the approval accorded by the FIPB.* The automatic route means that foreign investors only need to inform the RBI within 30 days of bringing in their investment (in form FNC1) and again within 30 days of issuing any shares. Companies getting foreign investment approval through FIPB route *do not require any further clearance from RBI for the purpose of receiving inward remittance and issue of shares to foreign investors,* since the RBI has granted general permission under FEMA in respect to proposals approved by the Government (FIPB). Such companies are, however, required to notify the regional office concerned of the RBI of receipt of inward remittance within 30 days of such receipt and again within 30 days of issue of shares to the foreign investor.

Under the small-scale policy, equity holding by other units including foreign equity in a small-scale undertaking is permissible up to 24 per cent. Furthermore, there is no bar on higher equity holding for foreign investment not reserved by SSI, if the unit does not belong to the reserved list of SSI and is willing to give up its small-scale status.

8.3.3.2 Entry Rules and Sectoral Caps on FDI

Although MNEs/OCBs enjoy the same status as domestic companies, they face restrictions by way of limitations imposed *in respect to holdings in different sectors vis-à-vis the domestic company.*

Apart from discrimination arising from sectoral caps on foreign equity holdings, the other differences between the foreign investor and a domestic investor arise from the followings:

(a) the foreign investor has to obtain FIPB approval in regard to all proposals in which the foreign collaborator has a previous venture/tie up in India;

(b) the foreign investor has to obtain FIPB approval in regard to all proposals relating to acquisition of existing shares in an Indian company/takeovers;

(c) mergers/amalgamation of companies require the approval of both the FIPB and the RBI.

(d) investment and returns are not freely repatriable in certain cases and is subject to conditions such as lock in period on original investment, dividend cap, foreign exchange.

Moreover, no Foreign Direct Investment (FDI) is allowed in Agriculture, including plantation (except for tea plantations).

The Group of Ministers (GoM) under the chairmanship of Minister of Commerce & Industry is the competent authority to take a view on the FDI policy, including sectoral caps. Besides the Commerce & Industry minister, the other members of the GoM comprise of the Minister for Power, Minister for Communication and Information Technology, Minister for Small Scale Industries and Minister for External Affairs.

8.3.3.3 WTO, TRIMS and FDI

Under the Trade Related Investment Measures (TRIMS) of WTO (1994), the member countries are required *to phase out performance requirements* especially in regard to the local content requirement and foreign exchange neutrality by 1.1.2000 for developing countries and by 1.1.2002 for least developed countries. Accordingly, India notified two TRIMS, viz., that relating to local content requirements in the production of certain pharmaceutical products and dividend-balancing requirement in the case of investment in 22 categories of consumer items *(Economic Survey, 1999).*

It is noteworthy that the TRIMS Agreement of WTO has a *built-in mechanism for review.* In the recently concluded Fourth Ministerial Conference at Doha (November 2000), developing countries could successfully defer implementation of TRIMS by *another two years.* The agreement would come up for consideration again during the Fifth Ministerial Conference.

8.3.4 SIA & FIPB

The Secretariat for Industrial Assistance (SIA) under the Department of Industrial Policy & Promotion in the Ministry of Commerce & Industry provides information and assistance to Indian and foreign companies in setting up industries and also assist them in finding out joint venture partners. It functions as *the Secretariat* of the Foreign Investment Implementation Authority (FIAA). Once a project has been approved/conceived, the FIAA helps them in obtaining the required clearances. It also sorts out operational problems through constitution of Fast Track Committees (FTCs).

The Foreign Investment Promotion Board (FIPB), on the other hand, is a committee of secretaries, with representations from Ministry of Finance, Ministry of External Affairs, Ministry of Small Scale Industries and Department of Commerce under the chairmanship of Secretary, Department of Industrial Policy & Promotion. The FIPB considers those projects, which require its approval. However, investments exceeding Rs.600 crore are required to get the approval of the Cabinet Committee on Foreign Investment (CCFI).

8.3.5 Foreign Technology Agreements

Foreign technology induction is encouraged both through FDI and through foreign technology agreements. India has one of the most liberal policy regimes in regard to technology agreements. Foreign technology collaborations are permitted either through automatic route or through FIPB.

Automatic approval: RBI accords automatic approval for all industries for foreign technology collaboration agreements subject to:

1. The lump sum payments not exceeding US$ 2 million
2. Royalty payable is limited to 5 per cent for domestic sales and 8 per cent for exports subject to total payment of 8 per cent on sales over a 10-year period.
3. The period for payment of royalty not exceeding 7 years from the date of commencement of commercial production, or 10 years from the date of agreement whichever is earlier.

FIPB Route: For the following categories, Government approval is necessary:

1. Proposals attracting compulsory licensing.
2. Items of manufacture reserved for the small-scale sector.
3. Proposals involving any previous joint venture or technology transfer/trade mark agreement in the same or allied field in India.
4. Extension of foreign technology collaboration agreements (including those cases which may have received automatic approval in the first instance).
5. Proposals not meeting any or all of the parameters for automatic approval.

The different components of foreign technology collaboration such as technical know-how fees, payment for design and drawing, payment for engineering service and royalty are eligible for approval through the automatic route, and by the Government. Payments for hiring of foreign technicians, deputation of Indian technicians abroad, and testing of indigenous raw material, products, indigenously developed technology in foreign countries are, however, governed by separate RBI procedures and rules and are not covered by the foreign technology collaboration approval. Similarly, payments for imports of plant and machinery and raw material are also not covered by the foreign technology collaboration approval for which RBI is the competent authority.

8.3.6 INTER-COUNTRY COMPARISON

Comparison of FDI Frameworks

	INDIA	MALAYSIA	S.KOREA	CHINA	BRAZIL
Openness	Largely automatic; small negative list; 100% FDI in most sectors; uniform application of policy; ownership restrictions in a few sectors; no min. cap in most sectors; freely repatriable; M&A policy considered restrictive	Heavy hands-on Government intervention; Positive list approach; prior approval; licensing; ownership restrictions, except for manufacturing; min. cap; free repatriability; M&A restrictive	Heavy hands-on Government intervention; Positive/ restricted/negative list; approval and notifying system; ownership restrictions in a few sectors; free repatriability; M&A market difficult	Heavy hands-on Government intervention; Permitted/ encouraged/restricted /negative list; special incentives for FDI; case by case approach; approval system; ownership restrictions in many sectors; min. cap; free repatriability; M&A restrictive	Small negative list; largely automatic; 100% FDI in most sectors; ownership restrictions in a few sectors; freely repatriable; no special restrictions on M&As by foreigners
FDI Legislation	Covered under FEMA	Separate legislation	Separate legislation	Separate legislation	No separate legislation
Technology Collaboration	Most liberal (rated No.1 in terms of ease of licensing	Restricted	Restricted	Restricted	Restricted
Empowered Body	FIPB (Small set to service FIPB)	MITI/MIDA Elaborate setup	KSIC Elaborate setup	Government Elaborate setup	Investe Brazil

8.4 Status of Special Economic Zones

The Special Economic Zones (SEZs) scheme was launched in April 2000 with the specific intend of providing an *internationally competitive and hassle free environment for exports.* Salient features of this scheme being:

a. Units may be set up in SEZs for trading, manufacture, re-conditioning, repair or service activity.

b. Units in SEZs enjoy relaxation in regard to Industrial Licensing, SSI reservation, FDI, FEMA and Customs and Excise Acts, in comparison to those in the Domestic Tariff Area (DTA).

c. Units in SEZs can import capital goods and raw materials duty free and may access the same from DTA from bonded warehouses without payment of duty.

d. Purchases of finished products from DTA to SEZs, to be on duties as applicable to imports. *Since such supplies from DTA would be regarded as 'deemed exports', they would be exempt from payment of central excise duty and central sales tax.*

e. Units in SEZ could sell 50 per cent of the FOB value of exports in the DTA subject to payment of applicable duties and fulfilment of minimum Net Foreign Exchange Earning (NFEE) requirement. Units in SEZs may further sell finished products to DTA, which are freely importable or are allowed against other import licenses.

f. Supplies affected in DTA *against payment in foreign exchange* shall be counted towards fulfilment of export performance and NFEE requirement.

g. Retention of 100 per cent of exports earnings in EEFC account and allowed for repatriation without any dividend-balancing requirement.

While the units in the SEZ have to be a net foreign exchange earner, there is no minimum net foreign exchange earning or export performance requirement. All activities of the SEZ units are, moreover, on self-certification and monitored by a Committee headed by the Development Commissioner. The SEZs could be set up in the public-private sector or by the State Government with a minimum area of not less than 1000 hectares. Four of the existing Export Promotion Zones (EPZs), namely, those at Santacruz (Maharashtra), Kandla and Surat (Gujarat) and Cochin (Kerala) have been converted into SEZs. Moreover, twelve new SEZs, namely, Positra (Gujarat), Nangunery (Tamil Nadu), Dronagiri (Maharashtra), Paradeep (Orissa), Kulpi (West Bengal), Bhadohi, Kanpur and Greater Noida (UP), Kakinada (Andhra Pradesh), Indore (MP) and Hassan (Karnataka) have been approved.

Cross Country Comparison of Selected EPZs

Country	No. of Zones	Incentives	Employment	Investor countries	Sectors	Labour laws	Workers organisations
Bangladesh	2 public EPZs; 3 public & 1 pvt EPZ Under construction	10 yr tax holiday duty free imports & exports	2.2 million*	South Korea, Bangladesh, Japan, Hong Kong	Garments, leather, shoes, electronics	EPZs exempt from Industrial relations ordinance	EPZs-trade union, strike prohibited
China	6 SEZs, 34 ETDZs	Govt. infrastructure (roads, ports, power), corporate tax 15%, full refund of taxes on profits re-invested, duty free imports & exports	18 million in foreign invested firms	Hong Kong, Taiwan, Japan, USA.	—	Flexible labour laws	Single trade unions
Malaysia	15 free industrial zones	—	—	Japan, Singapore, USA	—	Labour laws apply except. pioneer industries	Restrictions electronics and pioneer industries
Sri Lanka	6 EPZs	10-20 yr holiday for new, large export projects or thrust industries	Estimates range between 90000	South Korea, Hong Kong	Apparel services rubber	Labour laws apply	No trade unions present, zones have employee councils

* : includes employment in the in-bond garment sector

Source: UNCTAD, World Investment Report, 1999.

While the responsibility of providing basic infrastructure in SEZs rests upon the State Governments, the promoter of SEZ (whether public or private) enjoys: *(a) full freedom in allocation of developed plots on purely commercial basis, (b) full authority to provide services like water, electricity, security, restaurants, recreation etc. on commercial lines, (c) facility to develop township within SEZ with residential areas, markets, play grounds, clubs, recreation centers etc., (d) entitlements as provided in the Income-Tax Act.*

SEZs are being increasingly perceived as a major source of attracting FDI across the globe. It needs to be stressed that a large number of Free Trade Zones (FTZs)/Export Processing Zones(EPZs)/Special Economic Zones(SEZs) operating in the developing countries are aggressively competing with each other, thereby providing the foreign investors a choice to invest. China has been able to insulate foreign investment from domestic policy issues through FTZs/ EPZs, where foreign investment *gets special treatment in areas ranging from capital to labour to tax rates.*

8.5 Role of M&A and Disinvestment

Global FDI crossed the one trillion dollars in 2000 (US$ 1270.8 billion). 'Cross border mergers and acquisitions have dominated this trend, as transnational corporations take advantage of widespread liberalization and deregulation in an effort to gain market shares, consolidate operations, improve efficiency and dilute the cost associated with investing in research and development and information technology' (A.T Kearney, 2001). Although formation of regional groupings and the concern by consolidation have been the prime movers of the bulk of the cross-border M&A in the developed world, M&As have also emerged as the preferred mode of FDI inflows to the developing countries.

M&As have been one of the main channels through which FDI inflows are taking place in India. Although the share of M&A in the total FDI inflows was not so significant in earlier years, it has gone up to more than 40 per cent of FDI inflows since 1997. It has been further observed, 'around 60 per cent of the cross-border mergers and acquisitions (M&As) in India were in the manufacturing sector in the late 1980's, followed by about 32 per cent in the tertiary sector and less than 10 per cent in the primary sector. *The trend of cross-border M&As seems to have reversed between manufacturing and tertiary sector, the latter accounting for a little over 60 per cent in 1999 while the manufacturing sector's share has fallen below 40 per cent and the share of primary sector has been negligible.* The main reason behind the rising trend of M&As in the tertiary sector is the greater degree of liberalization of the services sectors particularly the financial services. In the manufacturing sector, the leaders were automobiles, pharmaceuticals, chemicals, food beverages and tobacco etc. In the primary sector, mining and petroleum, extraction of mineral oils and natural gas are the notable industries with the highest M&As'. *(RBI, Occasional Papers, Summer, 2000).*

It was also argued, 'Indian industries are undergoing structural changes in the post-liberalization period. Competitive pressures are high not only due to deregulation but also due to globalization... Along with the rise in number of M&A deals, the amount involved in such deals has risen over time. There was also an increase in the number of *open offers*, albeit at a lower pace'. Discussions in regard to M&As, assume added significance in view of the disinvestments policy of the Government of India vis-à-vis the strategically selected public sector units (PSUs) in the non core sector and the suggestion that India can attract over $ 49 billion FDI in the next five years through privatisation programme. *'For the sectors of focus, privatisation programmes could attract FDI of $ 13 billion in energy; $ 8.4 billion in telecom; and $ 5.9 billion in financial services'* (McKinsey, 2000).

In regard to the possible impact on the economy, two points of views are worth mentioning. According to one view if the acquisition/take-over of an existing company is by a foreign investor, this may subsequently dry up the demand for products from domestic industries linked to the acquired company (backward linkage) on account of the foreign investor switching over demand to its own subsidiaries located abroad. In other words, such a take-over of a domestic company *may cause of de-industrialization of the host economy* (Patnaik, 1994). According to the other view, however, M&As may supplement domestic savings in the same way as *Greenfield investments*, especially when domestic firms are not viable, losing ground in the new situation and therefore, *due for closure*. Cross-border M&As, in such cases may act as a "life saver" through bringing in new synergy of new management and better technology (Bhoi, 2000).

A closer examination of M&A in the different emerging markets, moreover, shows that while in the case of Brazil and Argentina, acquisitions occurred under majority share, (that is with acquisitions of more than 50% of share), in the case of China, acquisitions of significant magnitude took place within the ceiling of 26 per cent of equity ownership. The privatisation/ disinvestments programme pursued in a number of countries, both developed and developing, provided for the 'golden share' being retained by the government. The golden share, although being a minority share, gave the government nominee the right to "veto" any decision of the Board of Directors of a company if it was found not to be in the worker's/public interest. The Companies Act, 1956 (in India) provides that the voting rights of a foreign investor can be limited in order that control remains in the hands of Indian shareholders.

8.5.1 Takeover Code

While the provisions of Companies Act, 1956, govern mergers and amalgamations (of domestic companies), acquisition of companies comes under the provisions of Takeover Code of Stock Exchange Board of India (SEBI). *In the case of foreign companies, while share acquisitions/ takeovers require the approval of FIPB, mergers/amalgamation require the approval of both the FIPB and the RBI.* With the view to review the SEBI guidelines for acquisition of shares and takeovers, also referred to as the Takeover Code 1994, a committee chaired by Justice P.N.Bhagwati was appointed in November 1995. The Bhagwati Committee was reconstituted in 1998 to examine the provisions of *"Substantial Acquisition of Shares and Takeover Regulations, 1997"* relating to consolidation of holdings, threshold limit and acquisitions of companies during the offer period.

The Takeover Code, 1997 was thus amended in October, 1998 on the basis of the recommendations of the Committee.

The major recommendations of the Committee, inter alia, include, *revision of the threshold limit for applicability of the Code from 10 per cent acquisition to 15 per cent. The threshold limit of 2 per cent per annum for creeping acquisition was also raised to 5 per cent. The 5 per cent creeping acquisition limit has been further made applicable even to those investors holding above 51 per cent, but below 75 per cent stock of a company.* One of the major concerns about M & A is the concentration of market power. While structural changes in industry may be the need of hour on grounds of 'economies of scale' and to face international competition, if it leads to anticompetitive effects such as *raising of prices* soon after acquiring the competing company, it would adversely affect consumer welfare.

8.5.2 Competition Law and M&A

According to UNCTAD, United Nations (1997), 'Most interventions by competition authorities occur in the case of horizontal M&As between competitors. Typical scenarios likely to raise competition issues are:

- The acquiring firm was exporting to a market before it acquired a competing firm in the market, or a foreign firm that already controls one firm in the market acquires another.
- A foreign firm uses FDI to set up a major plant in a market, another firm does the same, and then the two agree to merge (or one takes over the other), thereby eliminating local competition between their two affiliates.
- When a foreign firm enters a market by means of a joint venture with a local firm, the issue arises as to whether the foreign firm would have been likely to have entered the market separately and competed with the local firm in the absence of the joint venture.
- The possibility that the acquiring firm will have an incentive to suppress rather than develop the competitive potential of the firm to be acquired.
- The merger of two foreign parent firms can sometimes create competition issues in countries other than the home or host countries of the merging firms, i.e., third countries.
- A parent firm acquires an enterprise abroad, which, as an independent entity, is (or could be) a source of competition for the domestic market.
- Investments likely to lead to, or augment, worldwide dominant positions. Such cases typically arise in situations in which a transaction affects product markets in which firms compete at the regional or global level.

The MRTP Act, 1969 deals with anti-competitive practices in a limited way. While an appeal could certainly be made *against unfair trade practices and against monopoly practices* to the MRTP Commission *(or the Consumer Courts under the Consumer Protection Act, 1986)*, the Commission cannot go beyond issuing an order of *cease of operation* or impose a nominal fine to the violating company. In other words, deterring orders like confiscation of assets or 'arrest and confinement' cannot be given. The anti-trust/anti monopoly laws in the country are found to be weak in comparison to those in the developed countries and needs to be strengthened.

8.6 Presentations and Suggestions

8.6.1 McKinsey & Company

Shri Sirish Sankhe made the presentation titled "Achieving a Quantum Leap in India's FDI" on behalf of McKinsey & Co. Shri Sankhe expressed the view that there exists a potential of attracting FDI into India to the tune of *$ 20 billion per annum*. This translates into $ 100 billion of FDI over a period of five years. Drawing lessons from other countries, he observed foreign direct investments have generally come into the three segments of: (a) the domestic sector (b) the export sector and (c) the privatized sector (that is, the public sector opened for privatisation).

TABLE – 8.5

Cross-border Mergers and Acquisitions (sales) and FDI inflows

(millions of dollars)

Years	1995		1996		1997		1998		1999		2000	
Country	M&A	FDI	M&A	FDI	M&A	FDI	M&A	FDI	M&A	FDI	M&A	FDI
China	403 (1.1)	35849	1906 (4.7)	40180	1856 (4.2)	44237	798 (1.8)	43751	2395 (5.9)	40319	2247 (5.5)	40772
Argentina	1869 (33.3)	5609	3611 (52.0)	6949	4635 (50.6)	9162	10396 (142.8)	7281	19407 (80.4)	24147	5273 (47.3)	11152
Brazil	1761 (32.2)	5475	6536 (62.3)	10496	12064 (64.4)	18743	29376 (103.1)	28480	9357 (29.8)	31362	23013 (68.6)	33547
India	276 (12.9)	2144	206 (8.0)	2591	1520 (42.1)	3613	361 (13.8)	2614	1044 (48.5)	2154	1219 (52.7)	2315

In regard to obstacles specific to each sector, he remarked while product market related barriers matter most for the domestic sector, infrastructure and labour laws related obstacles are adversely affecting the export sector. Similarly, it is the political resistance in regard to privatisation, which is the most important obstacle. He argued if these obstacles are removed, these sectors alone could attract FDI equal to $ 10 billion per annum.

An analysis of countries comparable to India shows that maximum FDI into Chile has gone into the energy sector, in Brazil into the telecom sector, in Poland into the food processing & beverages sector. He observed India too attracted large inflow of FDI in the automobile sector, once necessary reforms were put in place. *Requisite reforms over a period of five years promise to bring in FDI equal to $ 10 billion in the energy sector, $ 4.5 billion in the telecom sector, $ 1.5 billion in food processing, $ 3.66 billion in the financial sector, $ 49 billion in the privatized sector and $ 11 billion in the export led sector.*

Policy reforms in the power sector need to be directed to end the existing monopoly purchase model of State Electricity Boards; *thus, making it free to be sold by the manufactures to the end consumers directly*. Privatization could also bring in larger investments. Half the Indian states have still not set up the power regulators. In the oil sector there is a need for providing adequate infrastructure for exploration decision and aggressively putting attractive acreage up for bidding. To encourage LNG terminals and pipelines, the government should introduce a Gas Act to ensure clear regulation of the sector and set up an independent, empowered regulator to implement the rules.

Policy reforms in the telecom sector call for actions to ensure a suitable transparent regulatory regime with a level playing field that promotes competition. It should, moreover, avoid "shocks" like in the past, where basic licenses were granted in only a few states, or the regulatory authorities were suddenly reconstituted. Policy reforms in the financial services call for grant of fresh licenses to foreign banks, progressive reduction of CRR and SLR, reduction of priority sector landing and permission to mutual funds to manage provident funds.

Policy reforms in food processing and beverages call for creating a level playing field between small and larger players (although manufacture of bread, pickles and chutney may be reserved for SSI sector), and removing licensing and FDI restrictions. There is a need to reduce excise duty and sales tax and withdraw special exercise duty on food products, which are currently the highest in the world. Recent withdrawal of control orders in regard to storages as well as on restriction on movement of food grains should help bring in foreign investments in these sectors. In regard to retail trade, similarly, there is a need to allow full ownership through raising the limit to 100 per cent FDI.

In the export segment, the newly established SEZs should focus on: (a) closer proximity to ports and industrial hubs, (b) area extending to 50-100 square kms. to attract sizeable number of industries, (c) relaxed labour laws, (d) Independent Power Producers and (e) investment by Government in roads, ports, telecom. He remarked FDI has largely been responsible for contributing to China's runaway success in exports, which currently accounts for 40 per cent of total exports.

Shri Sankhey, further argued privatisation holds a big promise for attracting FDI to the tune of $ 10 billion per annum. In his view, the Cabinet Committee on Disinvestment responsible for policy strategy and targets *should set much more aggressive targets for privatisation.* Brazil has privatized most of the important sectors of the economy such as steel, railroad, telecom, utilities and ports. During the national privatisation programme in the country, the decision-making and implementation were kept separate, with the latter being handled by the Brazilian Development Bank. The barriers to privatisation arise mainly from (a) workers anxiety of losing jobs and (b) political resistance. While the worker's feeling may be assuaged through offering them free equity or at a discount, the latter issue could be addressed through making it obligatory upon the buyers to meet social goals. The Government of India, may similarly, constitute an apex body in the form of an Advisory Committee comprising of the CEOs of MNCs in the country to advise the Government.

8.6.2 A. T. Kearney

Dr. C. Srinivasan making the presentation on behalf of A T Kearney remarked he agreed entirely with the analysis of the McKinsey & Company in that there exists a high potential of attracting FDI into India. Today, even a country like Botswana attracts more FDI annually than India. The findings of his firm are based on the survey of 1000 MNCs, of which 250 responded to the questionnaire. The sample represents a well-informed group of respondents. Approximately, half of them have a positive outlook on India as an investment destination. More importantly, the current investors feel mostly positive about India, with over 40 per cent expressing a high likelihood of investing further in the next one to three years.

Respondents, generally identified *market size, labour force skills, competitive wages, government incentives and opportunities in infrastructure development* as the factors that distinguish India from other destinations for investment. Although ranked second after market size, India's skilled labour force has the potential for claiming the spot light as the country's most alluring characteristics for investment.

Whereas 25 per cent of foreign investors appeared attracted by the relative rates of returns, around 23 per cent of investors looked forward to accelerated implementation of promised reforms. Another 13 per cent of foreign investors attached importance to *India's image* as an export platform. The remaining investors perceived strategic alliances with foreign investors and improved government efficiency as important drivers to attract high foreign investment. Dr. Srinivasan suggested there was a need to take concrete steps in these directions.

Bureaucracy however, topped the list of investors concern. While three fourth of the respondents indicated that the investment process most affected by India's red tape *is the approval of an investment*, the remainder identified *project clearance as a hurdle.* The respondents also indicated that the divide between central and regional governments in the treatment of foreign investors could undermine the FDI promotion efforts of the Central Government. Dr. Srinivasan finally observed, there is a need to treat foreign investors as long-term partners, bring accountability into the economic system and have a one-model agency for project approval and project clearance.

8.6.3 Boston Consulting Group

Mr. Von Marsow Valentin made the presentation on behalf of the Boston Consulting Group (BCG). BCG observed, it is well known that FDI brings benefits through the export sector by way of linking the local economy to the international economy, through the infrastructure sector by increasing the overall efficiency and to the domestic sector through introduction of new products and services. All the three sectors, moreover, contribute in varying degrees in creating new employment opportunities, new technologies and new methods of doing business.

The numbers around FDI inflows into India are well documented; although these are just not good enough, have stagnated and are much less than China. There are good reports by AT Kearney relating to FDI confidence Index and by American Chambers of Commerce/ McKinsey & Company in regard to sector specific problems being faced by FDI in India. There is indeed a long list of recommendations on what India should do to attract larger inflow of FDI. According to the joint study of Harvard University and BCG, based on the in-depth interviews of 28 senior MNC executives across the globe, *there is a need to differentiate between 'problems of India' and 'problems of FDI'*. We also must not forget that unlike China or Singapore, India is a democracy and has a federal government. That does not mean that India cannot achieve results since democratic governments with federal structures like USA and Germany are success stories.

Economic Reforms have been introduced in India as is evident from changes since 1995 and 1998. In the perception of BCG necessary initiatives may be taken in the short run *within the given constraint*. The most important thing the Government must do is to really welcome FDI – show this welcome in their attitude and in the body language. There is an impression conveyed that foreign investors are trying to take something away and that there are hidden agendas. It ought to be recognized, moreover, that whenever a company outside thinks of making any new investment, *it goes through the four stages in the decision making process, namely, (a) screening, (b) planning, (c) implementing and (d) operating and expanding*. Unfortunately, India is out at the screening stage itself.

This happens because there are unhappy episodes going around about the business environment in India. The perception is that even before the foreign investor may even consider a project, he is already Enroned! The problem at the screening stage needs to be seriously addressed *through improving the image of India, marketing India and conveying a positive approach towards FDI to foreign investors.* Unhappy encounters should have to be replaced by success stories. India is, moreover, a multi-cultural society and most of the MNCs do not understand the different stakeholders in this country. There is, also, paucity of relevant data on areas of potential investment.

What is called for is a 'Rifle Shot approach' rather than the 'Scatter Shot approach' to woo the foreign investors. In other words, impression created should be: *'these guys mean business'* against that of *'these guys are nice but haven't organized themselves'.* More importantly, the difference lies in short listing the potential investors vis-à-vis shallow engagement of potential investors. The three things, which would further help, are (a) attention to government process and machinery, (b) improvement in infrastructure and (c) concentrated zones of FDI activity. A Council may also be set up comprising of senior Government officials and business leaders specially MNCs operating in India *to support companies considering FDI.*

Responding to observations, Mr. Valentin stated every investor might have his own list of recommendations. What has to be seen is what is feasible in the Indian conditions. The 'Rifle Shot approach' would be to identify the potential investor and address to his concerns. The Chairman, further observed, irrespective of other useful measures, which may be introduced, *there is an urgency to address the first funnel of screening, to attract FDI.* He then invited FICCI to make their presentation.

8.6.4 FICCI

Making the presentation on behalf of FICCI, Dr. Amit Mitra observed their findings are based on the FICCI study titled *"The Experience of Foreign Direct Investors in India".* The study based on the survey of 421 MNCs operating in India shows that foreign investors felt positive about the investment opportunity in India. As high as 87 per cent of them based their perception *on the high economic growth,* 97 per cent of them based their optimism on *skilled labour force,* 74 per cent of them found profitability between good to average and certainly much better than China. The study also indicates that *as many as 56 per cent of the MNCs are planning to expand their operations in India.* General Electric leads them all, as it had one company initially and owns now twenty-one companies.

Amongst the obstacles, the MNCs mentioned the followings: *(a) plethora of clearances, (b) archaic legislations, (c) center-state duality (d) weak database, (e) unhelpful (lower) bureaucracy (f) labour laws and (g) weak image.* Elaborating further he remarked, even setting up of a restaurant required no less than 38 clearances which goes up easily in the case of setting a factory. Some of the laws relating to essential commodities, food items (PFA) and drugs continue to be archaic. Similarly, the center-state duality creates difficulties not only at the approval stage but also at the project implementation stage. Thus, matters relating to environment clearances etc. come under the purview of the Centre. The bureaucracy in general is most unhelpful in extending infrastructural facilities to whichever project are to be set up. *All these lead to time and cost overruns.* At operational level, moreover, multiplicity of returns has to be filed on a monthly basis. However, when it comes to data management/ data base, records are not well maintained.

He, therefore, suggested the Government should go for eight urgent initiatives, namely, (i) empower states with regard to FDI, (ii) strengthen systems, procedures and data bases, (iii) develop 'fast track' clearance system for legal disputes, (iv) change the mind set of bureaucracy through HR practices, (v) encourage strong corporate strategies, (vi) develop basic infrastructure, (vii) maintain conducive policy conditions and (viii) improve India image through highlighting cases of successful FDIs. Elaborating, further, on empowering states, he said there is a need to have only one clear authority with reduced confusion. There should, moreover, be competition amongst states and they should own the projects.

The detailed case studies carried out for the select MNCs shows that Hyundai could jump over the hassles of approvals and clearances through acquiring an existing company and General Electric appears to be focused on developing core competence in India. Similarly, while Motorola is all set to leveraging India globally, Pepsi has developed strong linkages with agriculture. *In all, these companies have shown that there is value for money in India.* The Chairman complimented Dr. Mitra for concluding his observations on an encouraging note. He then invited Dr. Tarun Dass to make his presentation.

8.6.5 CII

Dr. Tarun Dass, making his presentation on behalf of CII observed, the liberalization programme undertaken in 1991 did lead to surge of FDI inflows into India. This was in response to deregulation of the industrial sector, which involved opening up of areas so far reserved for the public sector to private and foreign participation. FDI inflows to host countries are generally dependent on market size and rate of economic growth in the host country. It is indeed crazy to note that a country that is 5th largest in the world in terms of purchasing power is able to attract only a scanty sum of FDI. China, which has a GNP size 2.2 times of India, is able to attract 20 times the FDI inflow of India. Similarly, Singapore, which has a GNP size of only, 0.23 times compared to India, is able to attract 3.2 times the FDI inflow of India. Countries like Indonesia, Philippines, Thailand too attracts greater FDI given their market size compared to India.

The real problem in India lies in the low levels of realization of FDI inflows vis-à-vis the proposals cleared. Although the realization rate has improved to 45 per cent in 2000-01 compared to 21 per cent in 1997, it remains a serious problem. The precise reason for the low levels of realization is *the post approval procedures,* which has played havoc to project implementation. This is leading to loss of investors' confidence despite promises of a considerable market size. *The number of clearances for a typical power project is 43 at the Central Government level and 57 at the State Government level including the local administration.* Similarly, the number of clearances for a typical mining project is 37 at the Central Government level and 47 at the State Government level.

Though India's FDI policy is competitive in attracting proposals, the post approval clearance system (even when approved by FIPB & RBI route) has been very poor. Unlike India where project clearance has to be obtained at various federal and administrative levels, in competing countries like Malaysia, Thailand, Indonesia, China and Sri Lanka, a single agency deals with FDI clearance. Similarly, Philippines also offers one-stop auction centers where all clearances pertaining to project implementation are granted in a time bound manner. State's investment policies are so far limited to granting concessions and incentives to woo investors rather than streamlining their bureaucracies. There is an immediate need of instituting a single window clearance agency to facilitate faster, implementation of projects. *The focus should, therefore, be on developing a suitable structure and process of a single window agency.*

8.6.6 West Bengal and Andhra Pradesh Governments

Shri J. Sircar, Secretary, Commerce & Industry, Government of West Bengal in his presentation informed that FDI in West Bengal has primarily come in the petro-chemicals, power and telecom sectors from the three host regions, namely, Japan, Germany and USA. The best way to woo foreign investors is to match and marry specific sector under consideration with the special advantage the host country enjoys. The Chief Minister of West Bengal visited Japan recently and despite a recession in Japan he was given assurance of further investment in the state. The State Government, on its part, has put in place incentive schemes for mega projects including FDI. Task Forces on sectors like information technology, service sector and agro-industries have also been constituted.

The share of eastern and north-eastern India in total FDI has been around seven per cent; the share of West Bengal alone being four per cent. However, whenever a business delegation from outside visits India, it is taken on a fixed circuit of Mumbai-Delhi-Bangalore and Hyderabad to the determinant of equally good locations elsewhere. There is also a need to further improve the international linkages of these regions through increasing flights and airport facilities. West Bengal and eastern India on the whole have skilled manpower and are rich in natural resources; however, in the absence of requisite infrastructure development these advantages are not able to attract FDI. The State Government may, therefore, be allowed to directly negotiate with multi-lateral and bilateral agencies for infrastructure developments.

He further argued that if the Government of India could consider laying a gas pipeline from Myanmar to India through the continental self or through Tripura to West Bengal (in India), this would give boost to future investments in this region. The Government of India may, furthermore, remove complexities arising from sectoral caps on foreign equity holding and may also consult the State Governments while framing the FDI policy.

Making the presentation on behalf of the Government of Andhra Pradesh, Shri Binoy Kumar, Secretary (co-ordination) mentioned the Andhra Pradesh initiative was basically in two steps, namely (a) formulating the policy framework and (b) formulating the legal framework. With a view to attract FDI in infrastructure (mega) projects, the State Government thus approved in December, 2000 the Infrastructure Policy. This was subsequently backed by Andhra Pradesh Infrastructure Development Enabling Act, 2001. The Act was given wide publicity to solicit public opinion before its enactment. The Act provides for an *Infrastructure Authority* (IA) and *a Conciliation Board* (CB). Amongst its many functions, the IA may prescribe the time limits for clearances necessary for any project and also may decide issues pertaining to user levies. The CB, similarly, is a dispute resolution mechanism to be headed by a retired High Court Judge. In case there is still some dispute the petitioner may appeal to the High Court. Institution of CB would thus considerably reduce the burden on the judiciary and would also lead to speedier arbitration/conciliation. He, however, observed the scope of the Act is limited to items under the State List and does not cover most of the infrastructure projects like ports, airways, highways and telecommunication which come under the Central List of the Constitution of India. He, therefore, suggested for a similar enabling Act by the Govt. of India. This could especially be done for the SEZ as a starting point.

8.6.7 DIPP

In the sixth meeting of the Committee, the Department of Industrial Policy and Promotion (DIPP), presented their views on Foreign Direct Investment. They addressed the FDI issue in four parts: (i) existing domestic investment climate (ii) the FDI framework as existing now (iii) performance of FDI under this framework and (iv) the future strategy.

In their view, while macroeconomic fundamentals remain strong constraints remain on the investment front, which impede both domestic and foreign investment. These constraints are mainly high public debt, consolidated debt around 73 per cent of GDP, annual fiscal deficit of around 10 per cent, declining public investment and high percentage of non-performing assets. Nearly half of the bank deposits are in government securities.

According to the DIIP it is important to note that the FDI policy of India has undergone a change since 1991. From 35 high priority industries under the automatic route during the 1990s, the government today permits FDI in all activities under automatic route except for ownership restrictions in 14 industries on strategic and security grounds. No restrictions exist on foreign technology collaboration. The initial three-tier institutional framework of (FIPB-EFCI-CCFI) FIPC has now been brought down to a two-tier framework of (FIPB-CCEA) which is more transparent and time-bound. A Foreign Investment Implementation Authority has been also set up for investment facilitation. The NRIs/OCBs have been given concessions for investment in certain restricted sectors such as real estate, domestic airlines etc. They are allowed to invest without any upper limit under Schedule-4 and in sick industries.

A cross-country comparison of India's FDI policy with Malaysia, South Korea, China and Brazil shows that India has the most favourable FDI regime.

According to DIPP India faces following drawbacks in comparison to China namely (i) our approval mechanism is diffused (ii) FDI is yet to become a national priority (iii) our infrastructure is in a poor state and dependent on foreign investment for improvement. (iv) small scale reservation policy is a major impediment in integrating with international production system. (v) no special treatment for FDI is provided for (vi) India's share in global exports is low due to high trade barriers and low total factor productivity.

It was also pointed out by DIPP that India's FDI definition is not as per IMF definition. There is significant underreporting as it excludes reinvested earnings and inter-company debt transactions. In 2001 FDI inflows was around US$ 4.3 billion. Looking at the sector wise performance, the manufacturing sector accounts for less than 30 per cent of FDI inflows, unlike China where FDI inflows into manufacturing sector accounts for over 60 per cent, According to DIPP this is so on account of lack of international competitiveness and low total factor productivity because of poor infrastructure. Capital goods sector suffers from overcapacity. Investment in processed food is restricted due to excessive sectoral regulations.

The sectoral constraints affecting FDI are; in the case of petroleum and natural gas sector, the lack of attractive acreage and inadequate seismic data, in the case of the power sector the inability of the State Electricity Boards to pay, in the case of food processing the hindering factors are the inordinately long time in product clearances, high taxes and SSI reservation, in the case of financial services it is the restrictions on license to foreign banks, foreign ownership limit in insurance sector, high CRR,SLR and priority sector lending requirements.

In the opinion of DIPP, assuming an 8 per cent average growth in the Tenth plan period would require an annual FDI inflow of say US$ 7-8 billion. Sectoral FDI targets (including privatisation targets) need to be worked out, with full ownership of sectoral Ministries concerned, based on concrete policy measures to be undertaken. There is an overall potential to achieve US$ 100 billion over the next five years. Privatisation alone has a potential to absorb US$ 49 billion. Active participation of state governments is required in attracting FDI.

They also suggested a list of legislative measures for *investment promotion* viz; (i) an Investment Marketing Fund be created to assist Central Ministries and State Governments prepare robust investment promotion strategies based on national priorities (targets), international competitiveness, TNCs strategies and competitors' strategies. (ii) FIPC be activated and broad based with participation of State Governments' representatives, sectoral experts,

Industry Associations, Financial Institutions, CEOs of MNCs etc. (iii) DIPP will be the nodal agency to strengthen IP & ID cell and an Investment Marketing Committee be set up to prepare calendar of promotion of events based on best practices/global benchmarking. (iv) Invite participation of Industry Associations (v) Develop strategic overseas presence through bilateral/ multilateral arrangements (vi) enlarge the number of activities under automatic route (vii) FIPB be empowered to give initial Central Government level approvals (company incorporation, DGFT registration, customs & excise registration, income tax registration etc). (viii) An Investment Facilitation Fund be set up to help States set up structures, procedures and mechanisms for single window clearances (e.g. AP Infrastructure Development Enabling Ordinance, Rajasthan Empowered Committee etc). (ix) FIIA be empowered to fix time frame on completion of all documentation requirements (x) Country windows and nodal officer mechanisms be activated.

In regard to *concentrated FDI zone*, the DIPP has suggested the following measures: (i) An FDI Zone fund be created (ii) State funding of FDI zones be based on FDI performance index (iii) FDI zones should focus on *international production relocation* with world class infrastructure, flexible labour laws, single window clearances, no special fiscal incentives (iv) export oriented FDI to continue under SEZ scheme (v) Government of India seed capital to be promoted by State Governments with private sector participation.

8.6.8 Other Suggestions Received

Discussions have revealed that removal of certain sector specific foreign equity limits & conditions as having the greatest negative effect on FDI. Removal of these would have the greatest potential for increased FDI. One such study has therefore recommended the following:

a. FDI in petroleum retailing should be allowed without any investment link to refining,

b. Allow 51 per cent FDI in retail, real estate and commercial construction,

c. Foreign equity limit in Telecom should be raised to 74 per cent (from 49 per cent).

8.7 Andhra Pradesh Infrastructure Act

The Andhra Pradesh Infrastructure Development Enabling Act, 2001 (Act No. 36 of 2001).

An act to provide for the rapid development of physical and social infrastructure in the state and attract private sector participation in the designing, financing, construction, operation and maintenance of infrastructure projects in the state and provide a comprehensive legislation for, reducing administrative and procedural delays, identifying generic project risks, detailing various incentives, detailing the project delivery process, procedures for reconciliation of disputes and also to provide for other ancillary and incidental matters thereto with a view to presenting bankable projects to the private sector and improving level of infrastructure in the state of Andhra Pradesh and for matters connected therein or incidental thereto.

Be it enacted by the Legislative Assembly of the State of Andhra Pradesh in the Fifty second year of the Republic of India as follows:-

CHAPTER I

PRELIMINARY

1. Short title, extent, application and commencement:

(1) This Act may be called the Andhra Pradesh Infrastructure Development Enabling Act, 2001.

(2) It extends to the whole of the State of Andhra Pradesh.

(3) It shall apply to all Infrastructure Projects implemented through Public Private Partnership in the Sectors enumerated in Schedule III of the Act and to such other sectors as may be notified by the Government under the Act from time to time. The Act will not apply to any Infrastructure Project which is undertaken by any joint venture between the State or Central Government Departments or between the State or Central Government and any statutory body or between any statutory bodies or between the State or Central Government or statutory body and any Government Company or any Infrastructure Project which may be taken over by any private party or private sector undertaking upon privatisation or disinvestment by the State or Central Government or Government Agency or by any statutory corporation or any Government Company or any Infrastructure Project which does not involve fresh, new, additional Investment being made by a Private Sector Participant or any Infrastructure Project which is expressly notified to be excluded from the provisions of the Act by the Government.

(4) It shall be deemed to have come into force with effect on and from the 20 August, 2001.

2. **Definitions:** In this Act unless the context otherwise requires:

(a) "Act" means the Andhra Pradesh Infrastructure Development Enabling Act, 2001.

(b) "Best Effort" means best efforts made in the circumstances.

(c) "Bidder" means any entity including any Bidding Consortium, who has submitted a proposal to undertake an Infrastructure Project under Public Private Partnership.

(d) "Bidding Consortium" means if the proposal for the Project is made jointly by more than one entity, then such group of entities shall be referred to as a Bidding Consortium.

(e) "Categories of Projects" means categories specified in Schedule II of the Act and such other categories as may be notified by the Government from time to time.

(f) "Charges For Abuse Or Abuser Charges" means the levy of charges by the Infrastructure Authority on any Developer, if any Developer abuses any right accorded under the Concession Agreement, in the course of development, implementation, operation, maintenance, management and transfer of any Infrastructure Project, to the extent as may be specified in the Concession Agreement or such other agreement as may be Prescribed by the Government.

(g) "Company" means any entity incorporated by memorandum of association under the Companies Act, 1956 (Central Act I of 1956) or incorporated under any other statute or deemed to be incorporated under the laws of India or the laws of any other country of the world.

(h) "Concession Agreement" means a contract of the nature specified in Schedule I between the Developer and the State Government or Government Agency or the Local Authority relating to any Infrastructure Project or such other contract as may be Prescribed from time to time by the Government.

(i) "Conciliation Board" means the Conciliation Board established under Section 32 of the Act.

(j) "Construction" means any construction, reconstruction, rehabilitation, improvement, expansion, addition, alteration and related works and activities including supply of any equipment, materials, labour and services related to build or rehabilitate any Infrastructure Project comprising of physical structures or systems or commodities or for utilization of resources or provision of services.

(k) "Developer" means any Private Sector Participant who has entered into a contract for the Infrastructure Project with the Government or Government Agency or Local Authority under the Act.

(l) "Generic Risks" means circumstances that have the potential to adversely affect the development of a Project or interest of the participants to the Project or interest of the Government or Government Agency or Local Authority and in the nature of construction period risk, operation period risk, market and revenue risk, finance risk, legal risk and miscellaneous risks as enumerated in Schedule IV of the Act.

(m) "Government" means the State Government of Andhra Pradesh.

(n) "Government Agency" means any department of the Government or any corporation or body owned or controlled by the Government by reason of the Government holding not less then 51 per cent of paid-up share capital in such corporation or body.

(o) "Government Company" means any company in which not less than fifty-one per cent of the paid-up share capital is held by the Central Government, or by any State Government or Governments, or partly by the Central Government and partly by one or more State Governments and includes a company which is a subsidiary of a Government company as defined.

(p) "Fund" means the Infrastructure Projects Fund constituted under Section 54 of the Act.

(q) "Infrastructure Authority" means the Authority constituted under Section 3 of the Act.

(r) "Infrastructure" means public works relating to infrastructure for utilizing the natural resources and providing services by either public works of physical structure or systems for facilities or commodities or utilization of resources or provision of services.

(s) "Infrastructure Project or Project" means a project in the Sectors as notified under the Act by the Government.

(t) "Investment" means preliminary and pre-operative expenses, capital expenditure, lease on land and equipment, interest during construction, administrative expenses, all operating and maintenance expenses including expenses incurred on recovery of User Levies.

(u) "Lead Consortium Member" means in case of a Bidding consortium, that consortium member vested with the prime responsibility of developing a Project, holding not less than 26 per cent equity stake in the Bidding Consortium and also holding the highest equity stake amongst all other consortium members. In the event of two or more consortium members holding the highest equal equity stake, the Bidding Consortium shall clearly indicate in the Bid which consortium member is to be considered the Lead Consortium Member and the consortium member so indicated or named shall be the Lead Consortium Member.

(v) "Lender" means any financial institution or bank or any entity providing financial assistance with or without security or giving any advances to any Developer for completing or implementing any Project under the Act.

(w) "Linkage Infrastructure Project" means from any Project under the Act any road link to the nearest State highway, national highway or rail link or water transmission link to the nearest practical water source including an existing pipeline or canal or water body or sewerage link to the nearest practical sewerage transmission line or sewerage treatment facility or such other facility.

(x) "Mega Infrastructure Project" means any Project implemented or undertaken through Public Private Partnership under the Act requiring an Investment as may be Prescribed by the Infrastructure Authority.

(y) "Local Authority" means any Municipal Corporation or Municipal Council or any Panchayat or any other statutory body formed, elected or appointed for local self-Government.

(z) "Local Laws" means laws other than central laws and applicable to the State.

(aa) "Member" means a member of the Infrastructure Authority which includes the Chairman, the Vice Chairman and any other member of the Infrastructure Authority.

(bb) "Non Profit Organisation" means any organisation formed for promoting commerce, art, science, religion, charity or any other useful object and applies its income in promoting its objects and prohibits the payment of any dividend to its members and does not allow its corpus or income to be lent or advanced or diverted or utilized or exploited by its members or office bearers or any other company in which they or any of them may be interested or connected.

(cc) "Notification" means a notification published in the Andhra Pradesh Gazette and the word "notified" shall be construed accordingly.

(dd) "Person" shall include any company or association or body of individuals, whether incorporated or not.

(ee) "Polluter Charges" means levy of Prescribed charges by the Infrastructure Authority on any Developer, if any Developer pollutes the environment or does not adhere to the specifications and measures for environment preservation & conservation agreed under the contract with the Government or the Government Agency or the Local Authority or fails to stop polluting the environment within 30 days of receipt of notice in writing from the Infrastructure Authority or the Government Agency or the Local Authority..

(ff) "Prioritised Project" means any Project, which is notified by the Infrastructure Authority as a prioritised project under the Act.

(gg) "Private Sector Participant" means any person other than Central Government or State Government or Government Agency or any joint venture between Central Government or State Government Departments or any Statutory Body or Authority or Local Authority or any corporation or Company in which Central Government or State Government or Government Agency, Statutory Body or Authority or local body is holding not less than 51 per cent paid-up share capital.

(hh) "Prescribed" means Prescribed by rules or Regulations made under this Act.

(ii) "Prospective Lenders" means financial institutions, banks or any other entities of such project financing track record as may be prescribed, who in principle or agreeable to provide guarantees or finance to the Bidder under any of the financing documents.

(jj) "Public Private Partnership" means Investment by Private Sector Participant in an Infrastructure Project of the Government Agency or the Local Authority in the State.

(kk) "Regulations" means regulations made under Section 78 of the Act.

(ll) "Responsive Bid" means a bid from an eligible Bidder which complies with all the requirements prescribed by the tender documents or other documents as the case may be.

(mm) "Rules" means rules made under Section 79 of the Act.

(nn) "Sectors" means sectors as notified under Schedule III of the Act and as may be notified from time to time by the Government.

(oo) "Sector Regulator" means the regulatory authority for a Sector or Sectors as may be notified by the Government from time to time.

(pp) "Sole Bid" means when in competitive bidding process there is only one Responsive Bid received by the Government Agency or the Local Authority;

(qq) "State" means the State of Andhra Pradesh.

(rr) "State Support" means grant by the State of any administrative support, asset-based support, foregoing revenue benefits support, undertaking contingent liabilities by providing guarantees or financial support to the Developer as enumerated in Schedule V of the Act;

(ss) "Swiss Challenge Approach" means when a Private Sector Participant (Original Project Proponent) submits an Unsolicited or Suo-Motu proposal and draft contract principles for undertaking a category II Project, not already initiated by the Government Agency or the Local Authority and the Government Agency or the Local Authority then invites competitive counter proposals in such manner as may be Prescribed by the Government. The proposal and contract principles of the Original Project Proponent would be made available to any interested applicants; however, proprietary information contained in the original proposal shall remain confidential and will not be disclosed. The applicants then will have an opportunity to better the Original Project Proponent's proposal. If the Government finds one of the competing counter proposals more attractive, then the Original Project Proponent will be given the opportunity to match the competing counter proposal and win the Project. In case the Original Project Proponent is not able to match the more attractive and competing counter proposal, the Project is awarded to the Private Sector Participant, submitting the more attractive competing counter proposal;

(tt) "Unsolicited Or Suo-Motu Proposal" means a proposal in respect of a Project not already initiated by the Government or Government Agency or Local Authority and which proposal is submitted by any Private Sector Participant to the Government Agency or Local Authority in respect of any Infrastructure in the State supported by project specifications, technical, commercial and financial viability and prima facie evidence of the financial and technical ability of such Private Sector Participant to undertake such Project with full details of composition of the Private Sector Participant and his financial and business background; and

(uu) "User Levies" means the right or authority granted to the Developer by the Government Agency or the Local Authority to recover Investment and fair return on Investment and includes toll, fee, charge or benefit by any name..

Chapter II

Establishment, Conduct of Business and Employees of the Infrastructure Authority

3. Constitution of Infrastructure Authority:

(1) The Government may, by notification and with effect on and from such date as may be specified therein constitute an authority to be called "the Infrastructure Authority".

(2) The Authority constituted under sub-section (1) shall be a body corporate having perpetual succession and a common seal, with power to acquire, hold and dispose of property both movable and immovable to do all the things incidental to and necessary for the purposes of this Act and to contract and may by the said name sue and be sued.

(3) The headquarters of the Authority shall be at Hyderabad or at such other place as may be notified.

4. Composition of the Authority:

(1) The Authority shall consist of a Chairman, and such other members not exceeding 15 in the aggregate including ex-officio members.

(2) The Chief Secretary to the Government shall be the Chairperson of the Authority.

(3) The ex-officio members of the Authority shall be the following:

i. Secretary to the Government, Finance and Planning (Fin. Wing) Department.

ii. Secretary to Government, Transport, Roads and Buildings Department.

iii. Secretary to Government, Municipal Administration and Urban Development Department.

iv. Secretary to Government, Information Technology Department.

v. Vice-Chairman and Managing Director, A.P. Industrial Infrastructure Corporation.

vi. Director General, National Academy of Construction, Hyderabad.

(4) The Members other than those specified in sub-section (3) shall be appointed by the Government in the manner prescribed.

5. Term of Office of the Members:

Every Member other than the Ex-Officio member shall hold office during the pleasure of the Government.

6. Terms and Conditions of Service:

The term and conditions of service of the members of the Authority including the honoraria and the allowances to be paid to them shall be such as may be prescribed.

7. Meetings of the Authority:

The Authority shall meet at such times and places and observe such procedure in regard to transaction of business at the meetings including the quorum of as may be provided by the regulations.

8. Appointment of Officers and Staff of the Authority:

The Authority may appoint such officers and members of staff as it may require carrying out its functions and discharging its duties under this Act in such manner as may be prescribed.

9. Constitution of Committees:

(1) The Authority may, from time to time constitute such committee or committees consisting of such members for performing such of its functions as may be provided by the regulations.

(2) The Authority shall invite such persons from the fields of banking, commerce, industry, environment, law, technology and the like as may be nominated by the Government from time to time to assist the authority in carrying out its functions under this Act on such terms and conditions as may be prescribed.

10. Functions of the Infrastructure Authority:

The functions of the Infrastructure Authority shall be as follows:-

(a) to conceptualise and identify Projects and ensure their conformance to the objectives of the State;

(b) to receive and consider Projects under the Act from the Government or Government Agency or local authority and process the same;

(c) to advise the Government or the Government Agency or Local Authority as the case may be, on the Project and give recommendations or suggestions in that behalf;

(d) to co-ordinate between concerned department of the Government and Government Agency for a project;

(e) to monitor the competitive bidding process for Category II Projects and provide for course correction, if required;

(f) to provide enablers for Projects;

(g) to prioritise and categorise projects and to prepare a project shelf;

(h) to prepare road map for project development;

(i) to identify inter-sectoral linkages;

(j) to approve the terms of reference for consultancy assignments in Category II projects and the consultant selection process thereof;

(k) to decide financial support and approve allocation of contingent liabilities for projects;

(l) to recommend and approve bid documents, risk sharing principles and bid processes for Category II projects;

(m) to approve scale and scope of a suo-motu proposal or project undertaken through Swiss-Challenge Approach and to recommend modifications of a non financial nature if required;

(n) to resolve issues relating to project approval process;

(o) to prescribe time limits for clearances for any project;.

(p) to review periodically the status of clearances and ensure that clearances are accorded within specified time frames and grant clearances if not granted within time frames or if denied, as may be specified;

(q) to decide issues pertaining to user levies including but not limiting to prescribing mechanism and procedure for setting, revising, collecting and/or regulating user levies and to decide and settle disputes relating to user levies;

(r) to approve sectoral policies and model contract principles;

(s) to issue and/or amend guidelines needed to effectively implement the Act;

(t) to co-ordinate with sector regulator/s;

(u) to administer and manage the Fund and its assets;

(v) to co-ordinate execution of the projects with Government, Government Agency and Local Authority;

(w) to supervise or otherwise ensure adequate supervision over the execution, management and operation of project;

(x) to build public opinion;

(y) to fix and provide for recovery of fees, levies, tolls and charges as may be prescribed or specified from time to time;

(z) to levy and recover charges for abuse and polluter charges from the developer;

(aa) to prescribe regulations to regulate its own procedures;

(bb) to take all steps necessary for enforcing the provisions of the Act and realising the objectives of the Act.

11. Powers of the Infrastructure Authority:

(1) Notwithstanding anything contrary in any other Laws for the time being in force, the Infrastructure Authority shall have the power to grant any clearance or permission required for any project save and except sanction to the project by the Government as provided under this Act and such clearance or permission when granted shall be final, binding and conclusive on the concerned state level statutory bodies or administrative bodies or authorities as the case may be.

(2) Notwithstanding any thing contrary in any law for the time being in force, the Infrastructure Authority may give directions to any Government Agency or Local Authority or other authority or Developer or person with regard to implementation of any Project under the Act or for carrying out its functions under this Act and such Government Agency or Local Authority or other authority or Developer or Person shall be bound to comply with such directions.

(3) The Infrastructure Authority shall have power to call upon any Government Agency, Local Authority or any other body or authority or Developer or Person to furnish information, details, documents and particulars as may be required by the Infrastructure Authority in connection with or in relation to any Project, which such Government Agency, Local Authority or body or authority Developer or person shall furnish to the Infrastructure Authority without any delay or default.

(4) The Infrastructure Authority shall have power to inspect, visit, review, and monitor any Project and its implementation, execution, operation and management through its official or officials and the Persons in charge of project shall be bound to give full co-operation to the Infrastructure Authority.

(5) The Infrastructure Authority shall have all powers to enable it to carry out its functions under the Act.

12. Report to the Government:

The Infrastructure Authority shall submit quarterly report as regards its working and operation to the State Government.

CHAPTER III

INFRASTRUCTURE PROJECT DELIVERY PROCESS

13. Participation in Infrastructure Project:

Any private sector participant may participate in financing, construction, maintenance, operation and management of Infrastructure Projects covered under the Act.

14. Project Identification:

Either the Infrastructure Authority or the Government Agency or the Local Authority may identify or conceptualise any infrastructure project. If the Authority identifies or conceptualises any Infrastructure project, then the same will be referred by the Authority to the concerned Government Agency or the Local Authority for its consideration and further action. If the Government Agency or Local Authority identifies or conceptualises any infrastructure project, then the same will be referred to the Infrastructure Authority for its consideration, evaluation and further action as may be required.

15. Prioritisation of Projects:

The Infrastructure Authority will prioritise projects based on demand and supply gaps, inter-linkages and any other relevant parameters and create a project shelf.

16. Recommendations by the Infrastructure Authority:

The Government Agency or the Local Authority in accordance with the advice recommendations and suggestions of the Infrastructure Authority shall submit the Project to the Government along with the proposed concession agreement relating thereto for its consideration and sanction.

17. Sanction by the Government:

The Government shall consider the proposal submitted by the Government Agency or the Local Authority and the proposed Concession Agreement and either accept the proposal and concession agreement with or without modification or return the proposal and concession agreement to the Government Agency or the Local Authority for reconsideration or reject the proposal within such time as may be prescribed. The Government Agency or the Local Authority will take suitable action on the decision taken by the Government on the proposal and the concession agreement including revising and re-submitting the proposal and the concession agreement if returned by the Government for reconsideration by the Government Agency or the Local Authority.

Provided that if the Bidder whose proposal submitted for sanction is not in a position to implement the Project, the Government may at the request of the Government Agency or the Local Authority with the approval of the Infrastructure Authority consider the proposal of the Bidder offering the second most competitive bid for sanction.

18. Consultant Selection:

The Government Agency or the Local Authority shall ensure adequate competition in the consultant selection process for any project. They may, frame the terms of reference for consultant studies and in case of Category II projects and present the same for approval and modification, if necessary, by the Infrastructure Authority.

Provided that in case of such selection process, adequate weightage shall be given to the technical capabilities.

19. Developer Selection Processes:

The Government Agency or the Local Authority may adopt appropriate Developer selection process including any of the following processes, namely:

i. Direct Negotiations:

(i) The Government Agency or the Local Authority may directly negotiate with a Bidder for implementing:

(a) Category — I Projects initiated by a Bidder;

OR

(b) the projects which involve proprietary technology, or franchise which is exclusively available with the Bidder globally;

OR

(c) the projects where competitive bid process has earlier failed to identify a suitable Developer;

OR

(d) the projects in prescribed social infrastructure sectors where a Non-Profit Organisation seeks to develop a project;

OR

(e) a Linkage Infrastructure project with the concerned developer of Mega Infrastructure Project;

(ii) In case a developer is selected through direct negotiations the Government Agency or the Local Authority may renegotiate the financial offer or recommend that all subsequent procurement for the project is made through the competitive bidding procurement process, the cost of the project be determined after such competitive bidding procurement process, and renegotiate the financial offer based on the revised cost of the Project.

ii. Swiss Challenge Approach:

(i) The Swiss Challenge Approach will be followed in any project belonging to Category – II, initiated by a Private Sector Participant who is hereinafter referred to as 'Original Project Proponent', by a suo-motu proposal.

(ii) The Original Project Proponent must submit to the Government Agency or local authority:

(a) details of his technical, commercial, managerial and financial capability;

(b) technical, financial and commercial details of the proposal;

(c) principles of the Concession Agreement

(iii) The Government Agency or the Local Authority would first evaluate the Original Project Proponent's technical, commercial, managerial and financial capability as may be Prescribed and determine whether the Original Project Proponent's capabilities are adequate for undertaking the project.

(iv) The Government Agency or the Local Authority shall forward such suo-motu proposal to the Infrastructure Authority along with its evaluation within Prescribed time for the approval of the Infrastructure Authority.

(v) The Infrastructure Authority would then weigh the technical, commercial and financial aspects of the Original Project Proponent's proposal and the Concession Agreement, along with evaluation of the Project by the Government Agency or the Local Authority and ascertain if the scale and scope of the project is in line with the requirements of the State and whether the sharing of risks as proposed in the Concession Agreement is in conformity with the risk-sharing framework as adopted or proposed by the Government for similar projects if any and if the project is in conformity with long term objective of the Government.

(vi) If the Infrastructure Authority recommends any modification in the technical, scale, scope and risk sharing aspects of the proposal or the concession agreement, the Original Project Proponent will consider and incorporate the same and re-submit its proposal within prescribed time to the Government Agency or the Local Authority.

(vii) If the Infrastructure Authority finds merit in such suo-motu proposal the Infrastructure Authority will then require the Government Agency or the Local Authority to invite competing counter proposals using the Swiss Challenge Approach giving adequate notice as may be prescribed. The Original Project Proponent will be given an opportunity to match any competing counter proposals that may be superior to the proposal of the Original Project Proponent. In case the Original Project Proponent matches or improves on the competing counter proposal, the Project shall be awarded to the Original Project Proponent; other wise bidder making the competing counter proposal will be selected to execute the project.

(viii) In the event of the Project not being awarded to the Original Project Proponent and being awarded to any other Bidder, the Government Agency or the Local Authority will reimburse to the Original Project Proponent reasonable costs incurred for preparation of the suo-motu proposal and the Concession Agreement. The suo-motu proposal and the Concession Agreement prepared by the Original Project Proponent shall be the property of the Government Agency or the Local Authority as the case may be.

(ix) The reasonable costs of preparation of the suo-motu proposal and the Concession Agreement shall be determined as per the norms Prescribed by the Government, and shall be binding upon the Original Project Proponent.

iii. Competitive Bidding:

(i) Competitive bidding will be adopted in all Projects initiated by the Government Agency or the Local Authority. The notice inviting participation will be adequately publicised by the Government Agency or the Local Authority as may be Prescribed.

(ii) The bid process will be designed to assist and ascertain, technical, financial, managerial and commercial, capabilities of the Developer.

(iii) In case of a two stage process being adopted for a Mega Infrastructure Project, the Government Agency or the Local Authority may require all Bidders to obtain from their Prospective Lenders, financial terms, expectations regarding State Support, comments on the Concession Agreement and other project documents (hereinafter called "Deviations").

(iv) Any Deviations proposed shall be enclosed in a separate envelope and shall not be part of the envelope containing the financial or the commercial offer with regard to a Project. The procedure for determining the common set of Deviations and the effect to be given to such common set of Deviations shall be as may be Prescribed.

(v) All proposals shall be opened and evaluated at a common platform in a free and fair manner.

(vi) It will be open for the Government Agency or the Local Authority to adopt one or two stage process depending upon the complexity of the Project.

(vii) The Government Agency or the Local Authority will periodically inform the Infrastructure Authority of the progress of all Projects undertaken through a two-stage bid process.

20. Approval of Contract Principles:

In case a model contract for a Sector has not been adopted or in case there are Deviations proposed vis-à-vis the approved model contract for a Sector, then, the Infrastructure Authority will formulate or approve the contract principles as the case may be.

21. Selection Criteria:

The Government Agency or the Local Authority will first satisfy itself about the technical ability of the Developer to undertake and execute the Project and will follow:

(a) one or combination of one or more of the following criteria for Developer selection through competitive bidding in Build Own Operate and Transfer, Build Operate and Transfer and Build Own and Operate Projects:

- (i) Lowest bid in terms of the present value of user fees;
- (ii) Highest revenue share to the Government
- (iii) Highest up front fee
- (iv) Shortest concession period
- (v) Lowest present value of the subsidy
- (vi) Lowest capital cost and Operation & Management cost for Projects having a definite scope;
- (vii) Highest equity premium
- (viii) Quantum of State Support solicited in present value

(b) For Build Transfer, Build Lease and Transfer and Build Transfer and Lease Projects selection criteria used will be the lowest net present value of payments from the Government.

(c) Such other suitable selection criteria the Infrastructure Authority may allow or determine.

22. Treatment of Sole Bid:

In case of the competitive bidding process resulting into a Sole Bid, the Government Agency or the Local Authority shall in consultation with the Infrastructure Authority, either:

(i) Accept the Sole Bid

OR

(ii) re-negotiate the financial offer

OR

(iii) reject the Sole Bid;

23. Treatment of Limited Response:

In case the competitive bidding process does not generate sufficient response and if even a Sole Bid is not received, then the Government Agency or the Local Authority shall in consultation with the Infrastructure Authority either;

(i) modify either the pre-qualification criteria and/or the risk sharing provisions and restart the bid process;

OR

(ii) may cancel the competitive bid process;

OR

(iii) in case of (ii) above, may have direct negotiation with any Private Sector Participant;

24. Treatment of Bid Submitted by a Consortium:

(a) All proposals submitted by a Bidding Consortium shall enclose a memorandum of understanding, executed by all consortium members setting out the role of each of the consortium members and the proposed equity stake of each of the consortium members with regard to a Project.

(b) The Lead Consortium Member of a pre-qualified consortium cannot be replaced except with the prior permission of the Infrastructure Authority and which permission will be considered only in case of acquisition or merger of the Lead Consortium Member Company. Further, after a Bidding Consortium is selected to implement any Project, the Lead Consortium Member shall maintain a minimum equity stake of 26 per cent for a period of time, as specified in the Sector Policy or the Concession Agreement.

(c) Replacement of other consortium members may be permitted, provided the same is not prejudicial to the original strength of consortium as determined in course of the evaluation of original bid or proposal.

(d) Any change in the shareholding or composition of a consortium shall be with the approval of the Infrastructure Authority.

25. Speculative Bids:

The Government Agency or the Local Authority with the approval of the Infrastructure Authority will be entitled to treat the speculative or unrealistic bids as non-responsive and reject the same. By reason of any speculation or unrealistic bid or rejection of such bid, shall not necessarily lead to termination of the bid process. The Infrastructure Authority will prescribe the norms for determining the speculative or unrealistic bids.

26. No Negotiation on Financial or Commercial Proposal:

Save as otherwise provided in the Act, the Government, or the Government Agency or the Local Authority will not negotiate with the Bidder on the financial or commercial aspect of the proposal submitted by the Bidder.

27. Bid Security:

(i) The Bidder will be required to submit a bid security along with the proposal for undertaking the Infrastructure Project, the bid security amount will be determined based on the Project cost by the, Government Agency or the Local Authority.

(ii) The procedure for refund of bid security will be specified in the request for proposal. In any event, the bid security of unsuccessful Bidder would be returned within 30 calendar days from the date of selection of the Developer.

CHAPTER IV

GENERIC RISKS DISCLOSURE AND ALLOCATION, SECURITISATION, RIGHT OF LENDERS AND FACILITIES TO BE PROVIDED BY THE GOVERNMENT AGENCY OR THE LOCAL AUTHORITY

28. Generic Risks Disclosure and its Allocation and Treatment:

The Government Agency or the Local Authority will as far as possible disclose Generic Risks involved in a Project and a list of such Generic Risks along with allocation and treatment of such Generic Risks may be provided in the Concession Agreement or other contract to be entered into between the Government Agency or the Local Authority and the Developer. The Government Agency or the Local Authority will make optimum disclosure of the Generic Risks, however if any risk is not disclosed due to inadvertence or due to circumstances beyond the control of the Government Agency or the Local Authority, then the same shall not be a ground for any claim, demand or dispute by the Developer.

29. Facilitation of Securitisation:

The Government Agency or the Local Authority may facilitate a Developer to securitise Project receivables and Project assets in favour of Lenders subject to such terms as may be fixed by the Government or by the Infrastructure Authority to safeguard the successful implementation, completion, working, management and control of the Project.

30. Rights of Lenders:

The Lenders will be entitled to recover their dues from the Developer and Project receivables in the form of User Levies and in the event of default by the Developer in completing or implementing a Project, the Lenders will have the right to substitute the Developer with the consent of the Government and subject to the approval of such substituted Developer by the Government Agency or the Local Authority and by the Infrastructure Authority, on the same terms and conditions as applicable to the previous Developer or with such modifications as may be specifically approved by the Infrastructure Authority.

31. Facilities to be Provided by the Government Agency or the Local Authority:

The Government Agency or the Local Authority will provide all facilities to the Developer for obtaining statutory clearances at state level, for providing construction power and water at Project Site on such terms as may be Prescribed and provide Best Effort support for obtaining Central Government clearances and assistance in rehabilitation and resettlement activities if any incidental to the Project on such terms as may be Prescribed.

CHAPTER V

CONCILIATION BOARD

32. Establishment of Board:

The State Government may by notification, establish a Board to be called the "Conciliation Board" with effect from such date as may be specified.

33. Constitution of the Board:

The Board will comprise of 3 members and will have a retired High Court Judge acting as its Chairperson and two other members who shall be experts in the field of either infrastructure or finance or banking or law.

34. Headquarters:

The Board will have its permanent Headquarters at Hyderabad and the Board shall meet under the Chairpersonship of the Chairperson.

36. Term of Office of the Members:

Every member of the Board shall hold office for a term of 3 years from the date of appointment. The State Government shall be entitled to reappoint any Member or Members for one more term of 3 years.

36. Terms and Conditions of Appointment:

The terms and conditions of appointment, remuneration and perquisites of the members shall be such as may be prescribed by the Government.

37. Functions of the Board:

The functions of the Board shall be as follows:

(a) To assist the Government Agency, or Local Authority and any Developer in an independent and impartial manner to reach an amicable settlement of their disputes arising under the Act or the Concession Agreement;

(b) The Board shall be guided by principles of objectivity, fairness, obligations of the parties, the usages of the trade and the circumstances governing the disputes including the good business practice prevalent in the national and international field covered by the dispute between the parties;

(c) The Board may conduct the conciliation proceedings in such a manner as it may consider appropriate, taking into account the circumstances of the case, the wishes of the parties that may be expressed and for reaching a speedy settlement of the dispute;.

(d) The Board may, at any stage of the conciliation proceeding, make proposals for settlement of dispute. Such proposal need not be in writing and need not be accompanied by any statement of reasons therefor.

38. Administrative Assistance:

In order to facilitate the conduct of the conciliation proceedings, the Board with the consent of the parties, may arrange for administrative assistance by a suitable institution or person.

39. Powers of the Board Central Act 5 of 1908:

The Board shall have the same powers as are vested in a Civil Court under the Code of Civil Procedure, 1908 (Central Act 5 of 1908) while dealing with the conciliation proceedings in respect of the following matters, namely:-

(i) The summoning and enforcing the attendance of any party or witness and examining the witness on oath;

(ii) The discovery and production of any document or other material as evidence;

(iii) The reception of evidence on oath;

(iv) The requisitioning of the report of any body or any analysis or decision from the appropriate forum or laboratory or other relevant sources;

(v) The issuing of any commission for examining any witness;

(vi) The power to regulate its own procedure and Prescribe Rules;

(vii) Any other matter, which may be prescribed.

40. Judicial Proceeding. Central Act 45 of 1860. Central Act 2 of 1974:

Every proceeding before the Board shall be deemed to be a judicial proceeding within the meaning of Section 193 and Section 228 of the Indian Penal Code 1860 and the Board shall be deemed to be a Civil Court for the purpose of Section 195 and Chapter XIV of the Code of Criminal Procedure, 1973.

CHAPTER VI

CONCILIATION PROCEEDINGS

41. Application and Scope:

Any dispute, claim or difference arising out of or in connection with or in relation to any Concession Agreement or contract between the Government Agency or Local Authority on the one hand and the Developer on the other hand, shall as far as possible, be amicably settled between the parties. In the event of any dispute, claim or difference not being amicably resolved, such dispute, claim or difference shall be referred to the Conciliation Board.

42. Commencement of Conciliation Proceedings:

(i) The party initiating Conciliation shall send to the other party a written invitation to conciliate under this part, briefly identifying the subject matter of the dispute, claim and/or difference. The party initiating Conciliation shall file the invitation with the Board in such Form as may be Prescribed.

(ii) The conciliation proceedings shall commence when the other party receives the written invitation from the party initiating Conciliation;

(iii) If the other party does not reply or does not participate in the conciliation proceedings, then the Board shall have power to call upon the other party to file its reply or give notice to the other party and proceed further without reply;

(iv) The Board may request each party to submit to it further written statement of their position and the facts and grounds in support thereof, supplemented by any document and other evidence as such party deems appropriate. The parties shall send a copy of such statement, documents and other evidence to the other party.

43. The Board and by Certain Enactments:

The provisions of Section 66 of The Arbitration and Conciliation Act, 1996 shall apply to the Board as regards the Code of Civil Procedure, 1908 and the Indian Evidence Act 1872.

44. Co-operation of the Parties with the Board:

The parties shall co-operate with the Board and in particular, shall comply with requests by the Board to submit written materials, give evidence and attend meetings.

45. Suggestions by Parties for Settlement of Dispute:

Each party may on his own initiative or at the invitation of the Board, submit to the Board suggestions for the settlement of the dispute.

46. Settlement Agreement:

1. When it appears to the Board that there exists a possibility of a settlement, the terms and conditions of which may be acceptable to the parties, the Board shall formulate the terms and conditions of the possible settlement and submit the same to the parties for their observations. After receiving the observations of the parties, if any, the Board may reformulate the terms and conditions of the possible settlement.
2. If the parties reach agreement on a settlement of the dispute, they may draw up and sign a written settlement agreement. If requested by the parties, the Board may draw up or assist the parties in drawing up the settlement agreement.
3. When the parties sign the settlement agreement, it shall be final and binding on the parties and persons claiming under them respectively.
4. The Board shall authenticate the settlement agreement and furnish a copy thereof to each of the parties.

47. Status and Effect of Settlement Agreement:

The settlement agreement shall have the same status and effect as if it is an arbitral award on agreed terms on the substance of the dispute rendered by an arbitral tribunal under Section 30 of The Arbitration and Conciliation Act, 1996 or its amendment or re-enactment as the case may be.

48. Termination of Conciliation Proceedings:

The conciliation proceedings shall be terminated:-

(a) by the signing of the settlement agreement by the parties, on the date of the agreement; or

(b) by an order of the Board, after consultation with the parties, to the effect that further efforts at conciliation are no longer justified, on the date of the order; or

(c) by a written communication of the parties jointly addressed to the Board to the effect that the conciliation proceedings are terminated on the date of the communication; or

(d) on the expiry of the period of 3 months from the date of the commencement of the conciliation proceedings. If the parties to conciliation proceedings request in writing to continue conciliation, such conciliation proceedings shall stand terminated on the expiry of period of 90 days from the date of such joint communication in writing to the Board requesting Board to continue conciliation.

49. Resort to Arbitral or Judicial Proceedings:

(1) The parties shall not initiate during the conciliation proceedings any arbitral or

judicial proceedings in respect of any dispute, claim or difference i.e. the subject matter of the conciliation proceedings;

(2) Notwithstanding the provisions of Sub-section (1) herein the party may initiate arbitral or judicial proceedings, where, in his opinion, such proceedings are necessary for preserving his rights during the conciliation proceedings.

50. Commencement of Arbitral or Judicial Proceedings:

No party shall commence any arbitral or judicial proceedings in respect of any dispute, claim or difference arising out of or in connection with or in relation to any contract or Concession Agreement, without first initiating the conciliation proceedings and commencing the conciliation proceedings by sending to the other party a written invitation to conciliate and filing the same with the Board.

51. Costs:

(1) Upon termination of the conciliation proceedings the Board shall fix the costs of the conciliation and give written notice thereof to the parties.

(2) For the purpose of sub-section (1) "costs" means reasonable costs relating to:-

(a) the fees of the Board as may be prescribed and expenses of the Board and witnesses requested by the Board with the consent of the parties;

(b) any expert advice requested by the Board with the consent of the parties;

(c) any assistance provided, by the Conciliation Board;

(d) any other expenses incurred in connection with the conciliation proceedings and the settlement agreement.

(3) The costs shall be borne equally by the parties unless the Settlement agreement provides for a different apportionment. All other expenses incurred by a party shall be borne by that party.

52. Deposits:

(1) The Board may direct each party to deposit an equal amount as an advance for the costs referred to in Sub-section (2) of Section (51), which the Board expects will be incurred.

(2) During the course of the conciliation proceedings, the Board may direct supplementary deposits in an equal amount from each party.

(3) If the required deposits under Sub-sections (1) and (2) are not paid in full by the parties within thirty days of the direction, the Board may suspend the proceedings or may make a written order of termination of the proceedings to the parties, effective on the date of that order.

(4) Upon termination of the conciliation proceedings, the Board shall render an

account to the parties of the deposits received and shall return any unexpended balance to the parties.

53. Admissibility of Evidence in other Proceedings Central Act no. 26 of 1996:

The Provisions of Section 81 of The Arbitration and Conciliation Act, 1996 shall apply to the matters before the Board relating to admissibility of evidence in other proceedings.

Chapter VII

Infrastructure Projects Fund

54. Establishment of the Fund:

The Government shall establish a Fund to be called the "Infrastructure Projects Fund" and shall contribute a sum of Rs.100 lakhs to the Fund. The Government will make such further contributions to the Fund as it may deem appropriate from time to time.

55. Fees and Charges to be Credited to the Fund:

The Government Agency or the Local Authority will interalia levy fees and charges on the application for Projects and Project fee on the Developer under the Concession Agreement as may be prescribed from time to time and which fees shall be credited to the Fund.

56. Administration of the Fund:

The Fund will be administered and managed by the Infrastructure Authority and the Infrastructure Authority will be entitled to appoint an officer or officers for the management, control and administration of the Fund.

57. Utilisation of the Fund:

The Infrastructure Authority will utilise the Fund for achieving objects and purposes of this Act and for financing the activities of the Infrastructure Authority for realising the objects and purposes of the Act, time to time.

58. Operation of the Fund:

The Fund will be operated by and under the name of the Infrastructure Authority.

59. Formulation of Policy & Regulations for the Fund:

The Infrastructure Authority shall formulate its policy and regulations for financing, working, administration and management of the Fund.

60. Audit Report of the Fund:

The working of the Fund shall be subject to audit by Comptroller and Auditor General and the Infrastructure Authority shall submit a report every year as regards the working and operation of the Fund, to the State Government who will present the same before the Legislative Assembly of the State.

CHAPTER VIII

MISCELLANEOUS

61. Control by Government:

(1) The Infrastructure Authority shall exercise its powers and perform its functioning under the Act in accordance with the policy framed and guidelines laid down from time to time, by the Government and it shall be bound to comply with such directions, which may be issued, from time to time, by the Government for efficient administration and effective implementation of the Act.

(2) If, in connection with the exercise of the powers and the performance of the functions of the Infrastructure Authority under the Act, any dispute arises between the Infrastructure Authority and the Government, the Government shall decide the matter and the Government's decision shall be final.

62. Transparency:

The Infrastructure Authority shall ensure transparency while exercising its powers and discharging its functions.

63. Abuser Charges:

(1) The Infrastructure Authority shall be entitled to levy Abuser Charges for abuse, on the Developer, if any Developer abuses the rights granted to the Developer under the Concession Agreement. Provided the Infrastructure Authority shall give an opportunity of not less than fifteen days from the date of service of a notice to the Developer to show cause in writing, why such Abuser Charges should not be levied on him, before passing the order under this section.

(2) The Concession Agreement will provide what will constitute abuse of rights granted to the Developer. The Abuser Charges will be as prescribed by the Infrastructure Authority from time to time. Provided that the Abuser charges levied under this Section shall be final and conclusive subject to provisions of section 66 of the Act.

64. Polluter Charges:

(1) The Infrastructure Authority shall be entitled to levy Polluter Charges for pollution of the environment on the Developer, if the Developer pollutes the environment and/or does not adhere to the specified mitigation measures as provided in the Concession Agreement.

(2) The Infrastructure Authority shall give an opportunity of not less than fifteen days from the date of service of a notice to the Developer to show cause, in writing, why such Polluter Charges should not be levied on the Developer, before passing the order under this Section.

(3) The Polluter Charges will be as Prescribed by the Infrastructure Authority; Provided that the Polluter Charges levied under this Section shall be final and conclusive subject to provisions of section 66 of the Act.

65. Appeal:

(1) An Appeal shall lie to the Government against the order passed by the Infrastructure Authority under section 11, 63 and/or section 64 of the Act within 30 days from the date of receipt of the Order subject to the rules prescribed by the Government in this regard.

(2) The decision of the Government under sub-section (1) shall be final and conclusive.

66. Indemnity by the Developer:

The Developer shall be bound to indemnify the Government Agency or the Local Authority against any defect in design, construction, maintenance and operation of the Project and shall undertake to reimburse all costs, charges, expenses, losses and damages in that behalf.

67. Recovery of Costs, Charges, Dues Fees, and Fines:

The Infrastructure Authority or the Government Agency or the Local Authority or the Conciliation Board shall be entitled to recover all sums due to it under the Act, whether by way of costs, charges dues, fees or fines, in accordance with the provisions of the Andhra Pradesh Revenue Recovery Act, 1864 as if any such sum may be recovered in the same manner as arrear of land revenue under the provisions of the said Act and remit the same to the Infrastructure Projects Fund as it may direct.

68. Application of Fines and Charges:

The Infrastructure Authority or the Government Agency or the Local Authority or the Conciliation Board imposing the costs, charges, fees and fine under the Act may direct that the whole or any part thereof shall be applicable towards payment of the costs of the proceedings.

69. Penalties:

(i) Whoever fails or omits to comply with or contravenes any of the provisions of the Act or order or directions of the Infrastructure Authority shall be liable for each of such failure or omission or contravention for fine which shall not be less than Rs.50,000/- (Rupees Fifty thousand) but which may extend up to Rs.100,00,000/- (Rupees One Crore) or shall be punishable with imprisonment for a term which shall not be less than one month but which may extend to three years or with both.

(ii) Whoever fails or omits to comply with or contravenes any of the provisions of the Act or order or directions of the Board shall be liable for each of such failure or omission or contravention for fine which shall not be less then Rs.50,000/-(Rupees Fifty thousand) but which may extend up to Rs.1,00,00,000/- (Rupees One Crore) or shall be punishable with imprisonment for a term which shall not be less than one month but which may extend to two years or with both.

70. Offences by Companies:

(1) Where an offence under the Act has been committed by a company every person who at the time when the offence was committed, was in charge of, and was responsible to the company for the conduct of the business of the company, as well as the company, shall be deemed to be guilty of the offence and shall be liable to be proceeded against and punished accordingly.

Provided that nothing contained in this sub-section shall render any such person liable to any punishment if he proves that the offence was committed without his knowledge or that he had exercised all due diligence to prevent the Commission of such an offence.

(2) Notwithstanding anything contained in sub-section (1), wherein an offence under this Act, has been committed by a company and it is proved that the offence has been committed with the consent or connivance of, or is attributable to any neglect on the part of, any director, manager, secretary or other officer of the company, such director, manager, secretary or other officer shall be deemed to be guilty of that offence and shall be liable to be proceeded against and punished accordingly.

For the purposes of this section:

(a) "Company" means a body corporate and includes a firm or other association of individuals; and

(b) "Director" in relation to a firm, means a partner in the firm,

71. Power to Compound Offences:

The Infrastructure Authority and the Conciliation Board may for reasons to be recorded in writing either before or after the institution of proceedings compound any offence relating to contravention of any provisions of the Act or order made by it.

72. Cognisance of Offences:

(1) No Court shall take cognisance of any offence punishable under the Act except upon a complaint in writing made by an officer of the Infrastructure Authority or the Conciliation Board generally or specially authorized in this behalf by the Infrastructure Authority or Conciliation Board as the case may be and no Court other than the Metropolitan Magistrate or a Judicial Magistrate of First Class or a Court superior thereto shall try any such offence.

(2) The Court may, if it sees reasons so to do, dispense with the personal attendance of the Officer of the Infrastructure Authority or the Conciliation Board filing the complaint.

73. Penalties and Proceedings not to Prejudice other Actions:

The proceedings and actions under this Act against a person contravening the provisions of the Act or orders passed by the Infrastructure Authority or the Conciliation Board shall be in addition to and without prejudice to actions that may be initiated under other Acts.

74. Protection of Action Taken in Good Faith:

No suit, claim or other legal proceedings shall lie against the Infrastructure Authority or Conciliation Board or the Chairman or other members of the Infrastructure Authority or Conciliation Board or the staff or representatives of the Infrastructure Authority or Conciliation Board in respect of anything which is in good faith done or intended to be done under the Act or any Rules or Regulations or orders made there under.

75. Members and Staff of Infrastructure Authority or Conciliation Board to be Public Servants Central Act 45 of 1860:

The Chairman, other members and officers and other employees of the Infrastructure Authority or Conciliation Board appointed for carrying out the objects and purposes of the Act shall be deemed to be public servants within the meaning of Section 21 of the Indian Penal Code, 1860.

76. Bar of Jurisdiction:

Any order or proceedings under the Act including but not limiting to any notification of a Project as Infrastructure Project, categorisation or prioritisation of Projects, Concession Agreement, bid process, selection of Developer, modification of any proposal, sanction of any proposal, implementation and execution of any Project, actions of Infrastructure Authority, actions of the Government or the Government Agency or the Local Authority, actions of the Board, grievance or objection of any party or person or group in respect of any Infrastructure Project, validity, legality, efficacy of any action or decision in respect of any Infrastructure Project of Infrastructure Authority or the Government or the Board, dispute settlement or dispute resolution in respect of any matters under the Act shall be heard only by the High Court and by no other court or courts subordinate to the High Court.

77. Power to Remove Difficulties:

(1) If any difficulty arises in giving effect to the provisions of the Act or the rules, regulations, scheme or orders made hereunder, the State Government may by order published in the Official Gazette, make such provision, not inconsistent with the provisions of the Act as appears to it to be necessary or expedient for removing the difficulty.

(2) All orders made under Sub-section (1) shall, as soon as may be after they are made, be placed on the table of the Legislative Assembly of the State and shall be subject to such modification by way of amendments or repeal as the Legislative Assembly may make either in the same session or in the next session.

78. Power to Make Regulations:

The Infrastructure Authority and Conciliation Board may make Regulations, with the approval of the Government, by notification in the Official Gazette, for the proper performance of their respective functions under the Act.

79. Power to Make Rules:

(1) The Government may by notification make Rules for carrying out all or any of the purposes of this Act.

(2) Every rule made under this Act shall be, immediately after it is made be laid before the Legislative Assembly of the State if it is in session, and if it is not in session, in the session immediately following for a total period of fourteen days which may be comprised in one session or in two successive sessions, and if, before the expiration of the session in which it is so laid or the session immediately following the Legislative Assembly agrees in making any modifications in the rule or in the annulment of the rule, the rule shall from the date on which the modification or the annulment is notified, have effect only in such modified form or shall stand annulled as the case may be, so however, that any such modification or annulment shall be without prejudice to the validity of anything previously done under the rule.

80. Delegation of Powers:

The Government may, by notification, direct that any power exercisable by the Government under the Act shall be exercisable by an officer of the Government, subject to such terms as may be specified in such notification.

81. Act to Override other State Laws:

If any provision contained in any State Act is repugnant to any provision contained in the Act, the provision contained in the Act shall prevail and the provision contained in any such State Act shall to the extent of repugnancy be void.

82. Repeal of Ordinance 4 of 2001:

The Andhra Pradesh Infrastructure Development Enabling Ordinance, 2001 is hereby repealed.

SCHEDULE I

[See Section 2 (h)]

The following Concession Agreement or arrangements with their variations and combinations may be arrived at by the Government Agency or the Local Authority for undertaking Infrastructure Projects. The arrangements enumerated hereinafter are indicative in nature and the Government Agency or the Local Authority shall be entitled to evolve and arrive at such Concession Agreement or arrangement incorporating any of the arrangements enumerated hereinafter or any other arrangements as may be found necessary or expedient for any specific Project.

(i) Build-and-Transfer (BT) — A contractual arrangement whereby the Developer undertakes the financing and construction of a given infrastructure or development facility and after its completion hands it over to the Government, Government Agency or the Local Authority. The Government, Government Agency or the Local Authority would reimburse the total Project investment, on the basis of an agreed schedule. This arrangement may be employed in the construction of any infrastructure or development Projects, including critical facilities, which for security or strategic reasons, must be operated directly by the Government or Government Agency or the Local Authority.

(ii) Build-Lease-and-Transfer (BLT) — A contractual arrangement whereby a Developer undertakes to finance and construct Infrastructure Project and upon its completion hands it over to the Government or Government Agency or the Local Authority concerned on a lease arrangement for a fixed period, after which ownership of the facility is automatically transferred to the Government or Government Agency or the Local Authority concerned.

(iii) Build-Operate-and-Transfer (BOT) — A contractual arrangement whereby the Developer undertakes the construction, including financing, of a given infrastructure facility, and the operation and maintenance thereof. The Developer operates the facility over a fixed term during which he is allowed to a charge facility users appropriate tolls, fees, rentals and charges not exceeding those proposed in the bid or as negotiated and incorporated in the Contract to enable the recovery of investment in the Project. The Developer transfers the facility to the Government or Government Agency or the Local Authority concerned at the end of the fixed term that shall be specified in the Concession Agreement. This shall include a supply-and-operate situation which is a Contractual arrangement whereby the supplier of equipment and machinery for a given infrastructure facility, if the interest of the Government, Government Agency or the Local Authority so requires, operates the facility providing in the process technology transfer and training to Government, Government Agency or the Local Authority nominated individuals.

(iv) Build-Own-and-Operate (BOO) — A contractual arrangement whereby a Developer is authorized to finance, construct, own, operate and maintain an Infrastructure or Development facility from which the Developer is allowed to recover this total investment by collecting user levies from facility users. Under this Project, the Developer owns the assets of the facility and may choose to assign its operation and maintenance to a facility operator. The Transfer of the facility to the Government, Government Agency or the Local Authority is not envisaged in this structure; however, the Government, Government Agency or Local Authority may terminate its obligations after specified time period.

(v) Build-Own-Operate-Transfer (BOOT) — A contractual arrangement whereby a Developer is authorised to finance, construct, maintain and operate a Project and whereby such Project is to vest in the Developer for a specified period. During the operation period, the Developer will be permitted to charge user levies specified in the Concession Agreement, to recover the investment made in the Project. The Developer is liable to transfer the Project to the Government, Government Agency or the Local Authority after the expiry of the specified period of operation.

(vi) Build-Transfer-and-Operate (BTO) — A contractual arrangement whereby the Government or Government Agency or the Local Authority contracts out an infrastructure facility to a Developer to construct the facility on a turn-key basis, assuming cost overruns, delays and specified performance risks. Once the facility is commissioned satisfactorily, the Developer is given the right to operate the facility and collect user levies under a Concession Agreement. The title of the facilities always vests with the Government, Government Agency or the Local Authority in this arrangement.

(vii) Contract-Add-and-Operate (CAO) — A contractual arrangement whereby the Developer adds to an existing infrastructure facility which it rents from the Government, Government Agency or the Local Authority and operates the expanded Project and collects user levies, to recover the investment over an agreed franchise period. There may or may not be a transfer arrangement with regard to the added facility provided by the Developer.

(viii) Develop-Operate-and-Transfer (DOT) — A contractual arrangement whereby favorable conditions external to a new Infrastructure Project which is to be built by a Developer are integrated into the BOT arrangement by giving that entity the right to develop adjoining property and thus, enjoy some of the benefits the investment creates such as higher property or rent values.

(ix) Rehabilitate-Operate-and-Transfer (ROT) — A contractual arrangement whereby and existing facility is handed over to the private sector to refurbish, operate (collect user levies in operation period to recover the Investment) and maintain for a franchise period, at the expiry of which the facility is turned over to the Government or Government Agency or the Local Authority. The term is also used to describe the purchase of an existing facility from abroad, importing, refurbishing, erecting and consuming it within the host country.

(x) Rehabilitate-Own-and-Operate (ROO) — A contractual arrangement whereby an existing facility is handed over to the Operator to refurbish and operate with no time limitation imposed on ownership. As long as the operator is not in violation of its franchise, it can continue to operate the facility and collect user levies in perpetuity.

Schedule II

[See Section 2 (e)]

Categories of Projects

All Infrastructure Projects may be categorized based on the extent of Government support required and the exclusivity of the rights granted. The Government Agency or the Local Authority with the approval of the Infrastructure Authority will be entitled to evolve any further category or categories of the Project having combination of categories as per the priority and other requirements of the Government Agency or the Local Authority. The Government Agency or the Local Authority with the approval of the Infrastructure Authority may divide the Projects into following categories:

1. Category — I Projects: shall be Projects where:

(i) no fiscal incentives in the form of contingent liabilities or financial incentives are required ;

(ii) the Project is viable even when land is granted at the market rates;

(iii) no exclusive rights are conferred on the Developer;

(iv) minimal inter-linkages are required.

2. Category — II Projects: shall be Projects where:

(i) Government or Government Agency will be required to provide asset support;

(ii) financial incentives in the form of contingent liabilities or direct financial support are required to be provided;

(iii) exclusive rights are conferred on the Developer;

(iv) extensive linkages i.e. support facilities for the project such as water connection etc. are needed.

SCHEDULE III

[(See Section 2(nn)]

Sectors

1. Roads (State Highways, Major District Roads, Other District Roads & Village Roads), Bridges and Bypasses
2. Health
3. Land reclamation
4. Canals, Dams
5. Water supply, treatment and distribution
6. Waste management
7. Sewerage, drainage
8. Public Markets
9. Trade Fair, Convention, Exhibition and Cultural Centres
10. Public buildings
11. Inland water transport
12. Gas and Gas Works
13. Sports and recreation infrastructure, public gardens and parks
14. Real Estate
15. Any other Projects or sectors as may be notified by the Government.

SCHEDULE IV

[See Section 2(l)]

Generic Risks

The Government Agency or the Local Authority will endeavour to disclose, allocate and provide for the treatment of the following risks in the Concession Agreement as may be applicable to a Project.

I. Construction Period Risks:

(i) Land Expropriation

(ii) Cost Overruns

(iii) Increase in Financing Cost

(iv) Time & Quality Risk

(v) Contractor Default

(vi) Default by the Developer.

(vii) Time, Cost & Scope of identified but related Work, and Variations.

(viii) Environmental Damage - Subsisting/On going.

II. Operation Period Risks:

(i) Government Agency Default.

(ii) Developer Default.

(iii) Termination of Concession Agreement by Infrastructure Authority or Government or Government Agency.

(iv) Environmental Damage - Ongoing.

(v) Labour Risk.

(vi) Technology Risk.

III. Market & Revenue Risks:

(i) Insufficient Income from User Levies.

(ii) Insufficient Demand for Facility.

IV. Finance Risks:

(i) Inflation.

(ii) Interest Rate.

(iii) Currency Risk.

V. Legal Risk:

(i) Changes in Law.

(ii) Title/Lease rights.

(iii) Security Structure.

(iv) Insolvency of Developer.

(v) Breach of Financing Documents.

VI. Miscellaneous Risks:

(i) Direct Political Force Majeure

(ii) In-direct Political Force Majeure.

(iii) Natural Force Majeure.

(iv) Sequestration.

(v) Exclusivity.

(vi) Development Approvals.

(vii) Adverse Government Action/In Action.

(viii) Provision of Utilities.

(ix) Increase in Taxes.

(x) Termination of Concession by the Government.

(xi) Payment Failure by the Government.

SCHEDULE V

[See Section 2(rr)]

State Support

The Government will consider the grant of following forms of State Support, ranked in its order of preferences i.e.:

(i) Administrative Support

(ii) Asset Support

(iii) Foregoing Revenue Streams

(iv) Guarantees for contingent liabilities and

(v) Financial Support

I. Administrative Support:

(i) The State Government will offer the following administrative support to all the Projects covered under the Act, namely:

(a) Provide State level statutory clearances within specified time limits after the Project is sanctioned in favour of the Developer.

(b) Automatically grant non-statutory State level clearances, if a Project meets specifications as may be prescribed.

(c) Provide Best Effort support for obtaining all central level clearances.

(d) Undertake all rehabilitation & resettlement activities and recover the cost from Developer.

(e) Provide construction power and water at Project site.

(f) Acquire land necessary for the Project, if the same does not already belong to the Government.

II. Asset Based Support:

(i) The State Government will offer asset based support to all Category II Projects covered under the Act. The Category I Projects will receive asset based support only if the sector policy specifically provides for the same. The asset based support comprises:

(a) Government owned land would be provided at concessional lease charges for Projects where ownership would revert to the Government, within a maximum period of 33 years from the date of grant of land.

(b) The State Government will commit/facilitate development of linkage Infrastructure for Projects.

III. Foregoing Revenue Streams:

(i) The Government will forego revenue streams in case of all Category II Projects. Government will forego revenue streams in case of Category I Projects only if the sector policy specifically provides for the same. Such support would be in the form of:

(a) Exemption of sales tax on all inputs required for Project construction.

(b) Exemption of stamp duty and registration fees on the first transfer of land, from the Government to the Developer and on Project agreements registered in the State.

(c) Exemption from payment of segniorage fees i.e. cess on minor minerals during construction period.

IV. Guarantees:

(i) The Government may guarantee receivables only in the case of Category II Projects, provided they are not collected directly from users.

(ii) The Government may also provide off take guarantees if it is the service distributor and is responsible for collection of user levies.

V. Financial Support:

(i) Direct financial support may be considered only in the case of Category II Projects.

(ii) The Government will have the final authority to approve direct financial support.

(iii) Infrastructure Authority will ensure that appropriate Project structuring will eliminate, to the extent possible, the need for financial support.

(iv) Extent of financial support will be used as one of the selection criteria whenever financial support is to be provided.